Breaking Free from the Shackles of Witchcraft

Sweda Whyte Crawford

ISBN 979-8-88943-654-6 (paperback)
ISBN 979-8-88943-655-3 (digital)

Christian Faith Publishing
832 Park Avenue
Meadville, PA 16335
www.christianfaithpublishing.com

All scriptures, except where indicated are taken from the King James Version of the Holy Bible and are used by permission. All other information written is my personal experience and message from the Holy Spirit for this end-time generation.

Printed in the United States of America

This spiritual guide tells us how to fight and defeat the invisible enemies without a sweat.

It teaches real-life strategies, using the Bible as the number one and only source of reference.

It contains simple yet still powerful spiritual warfare prayers taken from the Scriptures that, if practiced prayerfully, will set any captive free from the shackles of witchcraft and its curses in the name of Jesus the Christ.

CONTENTS

ACKNOWLEDGMENT

I use this opportunity to openly thank and acknowledge my Creator and Redeemer for the many experiences I had had while battling the many attacks of witchcraft. His victorious and delivering hands had granted me the amazing victory and afforded me to share this powerful book, *Breaking Free from the Shackles of Witchcraft*, with you in Jesus Christ.

Last but not least, I want to thank my two superheroes—my caring husband, Mario, and our smart son, Daniel—for their love and support especially during the time of my attacks and oppression.

INTRODUCTION

Breaking Free from the Shackles of Witchcraft is a powerful and dynamic book for everyone or anyone who has been held captive by this wicked and evil principality known as witchcraft. There are so many definitions for the word witchcraft. However, in a nutshell, witchcraft is an evil system that uses demonic powers to manipulate, control, kill, steal, and destroy one's life and divine destiny. The Bible is clear, it is through the power of knowledge that we will be delivered (Proverbs 11:9).

And this book offers powerful spiritual warfare knowledge and insights that are taken from the Word of God and guided by the Holy Spirit.

It was my very personal encounter with this wicked principality that led me to the Word of God, which in turn brought about my great deliverance from this evil spiritual being.

I am aware that many are challenged and overpowered by the spirit of witchcraft, especially in this generation. However, this is due to a lack of spiritual knowledge and understanding of the powerful Word of God, as stated in the law of Hosea 4:6, "My people are destroyed for lack of knowledge: because thou hast rejected knowledge, I will also reject thee, that thou shalt be no priest to me: seeing thou hast forgotten the law of thy God, I will also forget thy children."

Friends, witchcraft can only be overpowered through the powerful Word of God and an obedient life in Him. Keep reading this book to learn exactly how you can become free from the shackles of witchcraft in the powerful name of Jesus Christ.

CHAPTER 1

Witchcraft Manipulation on Our Health

Howbeit this kind goeth not out but by prayer and fasting.
—Matthew 17:21

There are many people, both Christians and non-Christians alike, who do not believe in the existence or the reality of the evil spirit of witchcraft. However, there are numerous scriptural references that talk specifically about this evil and wicked principality. It is the apostle Paul who boldly explained in the law of Colossians 2:15 that Jesus the Christ had already disarmed the spirit of witchcraft.

> *And having spoiled principalities and powers, he made a shew of them openly, triumphing over them in it.* (Colossians 2:15)

And now He, Jesus, gave all of us who are walking in obedience to divine authority the same power to disarm witchcraft, binding and casting him out of our lives in His name. God hates witchcraft and its works because witchcraft manipulates, controls, and destroys lives and destinies. Therefore, in the law of Micah 5, He reminds us that He is cutting such evil and its practices out of the hands of the wicked. "And I will cut off witchcrafts out of thine hand; and thou shalt have no more soothsayers" (Micah 5:12). A law of death is even sanctioned to all those who participate in and use the evil powers of witchcraft. Exodus 18:22 tells us, "Thou shalt not suffer a witch to live."

It is Jesus the Christ who helps us to understand that the evil spirit of witchcraft has different spiritual ranks. There are different levels on which this evil craft is ranked. And the law of Matthew 17 helps us to fully understand that a high-ranking witchcraft spirit is referred to as "this kind." However, Jesus did not just educate us on their ranks and their evil powers, but He also seeks to tell and show us how to get rid of such kind: "Howbeit this kind goeth not out but by prayer and fasting" (Matthew 17:21). Jesus gave us one of the most powerful warfare weapons against the high-ranking demon known as witchcraft or evil principality. We, the believers of Jesus, should fast and pray to get evil spirits out of our lives. But please note that Satan cannot cast out himself.

> *And if Satan cast out Satan, he is divided against himself; how shall then his kingdom stand?* (Matthew 12:26)

Hence, we also need to be living obedient lives unto God in order to truly defeat the enemy of witchcraft.

If we read carefully the law of Matthew 17:18, we will also observe the powerful showdown between Jesus the Christ and the evil spirit of witchcraft that was in a boy whom they labeled as *a lunatic.*

Matthew narrates the story powerfully as he tells it exactly as Jesus describes the evil high-ranking spirit of witchcraft that had been summoned from the moon to the life of an ignorant boy.

We know from Scripture that "this kind" was a lunar type because of the evil name tag *lunatic* that was worn by the boy, which gets its name from the moon.

In addition, the many occasions and time periods in which this evil spirit made dangerous attempts to kill the boy are usually when the moon is out or it's close to a full moon. So there is no doubt that this evil spirit's desire was to kill, steal, and destroy the life of the boy. The father of the boy describes the evil activities of the witchcraft spirit in his son's life very well in verse 15 of Matthew chapter 17. "Lord, have mercy on my son: for he is lunatick, and sore vexed: for ofttimes he falleth into the fire, and oft into the water" (Matthew 17:15). He, the father of the boy, gave a powerful summary of his son's situation, even though he was in ignorance, like many today, about the evil spirit of witchcraft that was sitting in the life of his son. I have seen this episode played out in my life also as I was a victim of such evil. However, the powerful hand of Jesus also reached out and grabbed me, and now I am free from the shackles of witchcraft. He, Jesus, rebuked and cast this evil wicked spirit of witchcraft out of the boy's life.

Moreover, the all-powerful hands of God reached out and touched the feeble body of the demoniac boy. Then power shifted hands, and immediately the boy was cured, according to Matthew 17:18.

> And Jesus rebuked the devil; and he departed
> out of him: and the child was cured from that very
> hour. (Matthew 17:18)

Catch this! Your sickness could be as a result of what the Bible refers to as "this kind"; and you can be healed in this hour by the power of the Word, who is Jesus the Christ.

Satan uses the spirit of witchcraft to manipulate the health of his victims. More than 90 percent of sicknesses and diseases have been caused by witchcraft manipulation from evil altars. When we study the Scriptures—also the works of Jesus the Christ while He was on earth, in the flesh—we get an understanding that everywhere He showed up, He needed to rebuke and cast out spirits of infirmity from many of the lives He encountered, as can be witnessed in the narrative of Matthew 9 below.

> And Jesus went about all the cities and villages,
> teaching in their synagogues, and preaching the gos-

*pel of the kingdom, and healing every sickness and
every disease among the people.* (Matthew 9:35)

Yes! It is a fact that medical practitioners are and will be the first
to rename what the Bible calls *this kind* as sickness. And you yourself
will even call that financial problem poverty. But God is telling you
that it is not what you think it is because the high-ranking demon
that is referred to as "this kind" is an evil summoned against your
health, your finances, or even your homes, families, and marriages.
It will continue to kill, steal, and destroy many lives and destines
because the "evil spirit of witchcraft" is also a robber who have not
been found in many lives, according to the law of Proverbs 6: "But if
he be found, he shall restore sevenfold; He shall give all the substance
of his house" (Proverbs 6:30b).

If you are a good reader of your Bible, you will discover that
everywhere Jesus went while He was in the physical body here on
earth, He encountered "this kind" in many people's lives. And because
He is the Word, He cast it out (see John 1:1). Jesus the Christ has
spiritual eyes that see beyond the problems. He sees the root cause
of the problems. He, Jesus, sees the demons that were causing the
problems in my life. Jesus dealt with the root as He uprooted the evil
trees of sickness, poverty, premature deaths, demons of sleeplessness,
and all other roots of wickedness that were standing in the way of
people's divine destinies as He ministered to them. Jesus the Christ
was activating the law of Matthew 15:13 as He disarmed all evil root
workers in the lives of many sick and diseased people.

*But he answered and said, Every plant, which
my heavenly Father hath not planted, shall be rooted
up.* (Matthew 15:13)

Everywhere Jesus went, deliverance was active, and the captives
were set free from the shackles of witchcraft in His name. The very
same can and will happen in our generation if men and women,
boys and girls would only seek spiritual knowledge and apply the
life-changing and lifesaving principles to their everyday lives.

All power truly belongs to our God!

I totally understand and know how it feels to have an evil root in my life. Yes! An evil root of sleeplessness as I was attacked by the spirit of witchcraft on the battlefield of life for many years before knowing what it was. This bewitchment had gotten so intense that it almost caused me to experience a close-up encounter with the spirit of death. Witchcraft had taken away my sleep for several years. I was a walking zombie before I learned the spiritual warfare principles to use on the battlefield of life.

I still can remember the moment like it was yesterday! For several nights, I would seek to go to bed in order to get at least an hour of sleep. I was desperate for even an hour of sleep, so I did not put my expectation very high of wanting more than an hour. But even that was a very high expectation because I would sleep off for twenty to thirty minutes, after which some unseen, evil, invisible hands would wake me up.

It was like I was an actor in a horror movie! How could this be with absolutely no medical help to cure this problem? I have been driven from one health-care practitioner to the next, from herbalist to acupuncture, from one masseuse to another, and with countless amounts of medication, hoping that one would at least help me to get some sleep. But it was a total waste of time, effort, and monies as my health was quickly deteriorating and my chance of survival was hanging in the balance, with a young son and a husband to think about at the time.

"There must be a God!" But I have prayed and worshipped. I had called several pastors (so I assumed) to pray for or with me, only to be told to call the crisis center. But my situation continued to get only worse. It was on one particular night, at about 9:45 p.m., that my husband had to call the ambulance as the evil altars began to speak louder (now I know). I had begun to urinate upon myself and my bed without feeling or knowing it.

It must have been the Lord Himself who had answered my many prayers and led me to a video on the internet; because there we found someone who had had a similar experience of witchcraft attacks (like myself in the past). Eagerly, my husband and I watched several of the videos, and I quickly followed the spiritual protocols by using the spiritual warfare weapons of fasting and prayers, along with obedience to divine instruction, to uproot the great evil altars of witchcraft that were planted in my life.

If we are good readers of our Bibles, we will quickly discover that witchcraft has been practiced all throughout the ages and it is even more prevalent in our generation. We are now living in the dangerous age of witchcraft, wherein people are using this evil spiritual being to kill, steal, and to destroy one another. The book of Nahum chapter 3 reveals the demonic activities of witchcraft, and it also tells us exactly what God thinks of it.

> *Woe to the bloody city! It is all full of lies and robbery; the prey departeth not; The noise of a whip, and the noise of the rattling of the wheels, and of the praccing horses, and of the jumping chariots. The horseman lifteth up both the bright sword and the glittering spear: and there is a multitude of slain, and a great number of carcases; and there is none end of their corpses; they stumble upon their corpses: Because of the multitude of the whoredoms of the well-favoured harlot, the mistress of witchcrafts, that selleth nations through her whoredoms, and families through her witchcrafts. Behold, I am against thee, saith the Lord of hosts; and I will discover thy skirts upon thy face, and I will shew the nations thy nakedness, and the kingdoms thy shame. And I will cast abominable filth upon thee, and make thee vile, and will set thee as a gazingstock.* (Nahum 3: 1–6)

It was Jezebel, the witch, who had demonstrated in showing us her evil powers of witchcraft in destroying the life of the ignorant Naboth, according to this powerful eye-opening story in 1 King 21:1–14.

And it came to pass after these things, that Naboth the Jezreelite had a vineyard, which was in Jezreel, hard by the palace of Ahab king of Samaria. And Ahab spake unto Naboth, saying, Give me thy vineyard, that I may have it for a garden of herbs, because it is near unto my house: and I will give thee for it a better vineyard than it; or, if it seem good to thee, I will give thee the worth of it in money. And Naboth said to Ahab, The Lord forbid it me, that I should give the inheritance of my fathers unto thee. And Ahab came into his house heavy and displeased because of the word which Naboth the Jezreelite had spoken to him: for he had said, I will not give thee the inheritance of my fathers. And he laid him down upon his bed, and turned away his face, and would eat no bread. But Jezebel his wife came to him, and said unto him, Why is thy spirit so sad, that thou eatest no bread? And he said unto her, Because I spake unto Naboth the Jezreelite, and said unto him, Give me thy vineyard for money; or else, if it please thee, I will give thee another vineyard for it: and he answered, I will not give thee my vineyard. And Jezebel his wife said unto him, Dost thou now govern the kingdom of Israel? arise, and eat bread, and let thine heart be merry: I will give thee the vineyard of Naboth the Jezreelite. So she wrote letters in Ahab's name, and sealed them with his seal, and sent the letters unto the elders and to the nobles that were in his city, dwelling with Naboth. And she wrote in the letters, saying, Proclaim a fast, and set Naboth on high among the people:

And set two men, sons of Belial, before him, to bear witness against him, saying, Thou didst blaspheme God and the king. And then carry him out, and stone him, that he may die. And the men of his city, even the elders and the nobles who were the

7

> *inhabitants in his city, did as Jezebel had sent unto them, and as it was written in the letters which she had sent unto them. They proclaimed a fast, and set Naboth on high among the people. And there came in two men, children of Belial, and sat before him: and the men of Belial witnessed against him, even against Naboth, in the presence of the people, saying, Naboth did blaspheme God and the king. Then they carried him forth out of the city, and stoned him with stones, that he died. Then they sent to Jezebel, saying, Naboth is stoned, and is dead. (1 Kings 21:1-14)*

However, in Revelation chapter 21, God tells us the final punishment for all those who engage in such abominable activities.

> *But the fearful, and unbelieving, and the abominable, and murderers, and whoremongers, and sorcerers, and idolaters, and all liars, shall have their part in the lake which burneth with fire and brimstone: which is the second death. (Revelation 21:8)*

Friends, ignorance of the laws in the Holy Bible can and will cause you to lose your life like Naboth and the thousands who have been victims of witchcraft, like myself in the past.

Balaam also used witchcraft. He specialized in raising evil altars to kill, steal, and destroy lives and destinies. Wizardry was a profession that Balaam took unto himself. But the Scriptures are clear, whom God blesses, let no man curse. So Balaam's twenty-one evil altars that were lifted against the children of Israel were total foolishness, as the curses from these evil altars could not manifest in the physical of any of their lives, as there were no sins found in Israel at the time as seen in the story of Numbers 23 below.

And Balaam said unto Balak, Build me here seven altars, and prepare me here seven oxen and seven rams. And Balak did as Balaam had spoken; and Balak and Balaam offered on every altar a bullock and a ram. And Balaam said unto Balak, Stand by thy burnt offering, and I will go: peradventure the Lord will come to meet me: and whatsoever he sheweth me I will tell thee. And he went to an high place. And God met Balaam: and he said unto him, I have prepared seven altars, and I have offered upon every altar a bullock and a ram. And the Lord put a word in Balaam's mouth, and said, Return unto Balak, and thus thou shalt speak. And he returned unto him, and, lo, he stood by his burnt sacrifice, he, and all the princes of Moab. And he took up his parable, and said, Balak the king of Moab hath brought me from Aram, out of the mountains of the east, saying, Come, curse me Jacob, and come, defy Israel. How shall I curse, whom God hath not cursed? or how shall I defy, whom the Lord hath not defied?

For from the top of the rocks I see him, and from the hills I behold him: lo, the people shall dwell alone, and shall not be reckoned among the nations. Who can count the dust of Jacob, and the number of the fourth part of Israel? Let me die the death of the righteous, and let my last end be like his! And Balak said unto Balaam, What hast thou done unto me? I took thee to curse mine enemies, and, behold, thou hast blessed them altogether. And he answered and said, Must I not take heed to speak that which the Lord hath put in my mouth? And Balak said unto him, Come, I pray thee, with me unto another place, from whence thou mayest see them: thou shalt see but the utmost part of them, and shalt not see them all: and curse me them from thence. And he brought him into the field of Zophim, to the top of Pisgah, and built seven altars, and offered a bullock and a ram on every altar. And he said unto Balak, Stand here by thy burnt offering, while I meet the Lord yonder. And the Lord met Balaam, and put a word in his mouth, and said, Go again unto Balak, and say thus. And when he came to him, behold, he stood by his burnt offering, and the princes of Moab with him. And Balak said unto him, What hath the Lord spoken? And he took up his parable, and said, Rise up, Balak, and hear; hearken unto me, thou son of Zippor: God is not a man, that he should lie; neither the son of man, that he should repent: hath he said, and shall he not do it? or hath he spoken, and shall he not make it good? Behold, I have received commandment to bless: and he hath blessed; and I cannot reverse it. He hath not beheld iniquity in Jacob, neither hath he seen perverseness in Israel: the Lord his God is with him, and the shout of a king is among them. God brought them out of Egypt; he hath as it were the strength of an unicorn. Surely there is no enchantment against Jacob, neither is there any divination against Israel: according to this time it shall be said of Jacob and of Israel, What hath God wrought! Behold, the people shall rise up as a great lion, and lift up himself as a young lion: he shall not lie down until he eat of the prey, and drink the blood of the slain. And Balak said unto Balaam, Neither curse them at all, nor bless them at all. But Balaam answered and said unto Balak, Told not I thee, saying, All that the Lord speaketh, that I must do? And Balak said unto Balaam, Come, I pray thee, I will bring thee unto another place; peradventure it will please God that thou mayest curse me them from thence. And Balak brought Balaam unto the top of Peor, that

*looketh toward jeshimon. And Balaam said unto
Balak, Build me here seven altars, and prepare me
here seven bullocks and seven rams. And Balak did
as Balaam had said, and offered a bullock and a
ram on every altar.* (Numbers 23:1–30)

From this powerful narrative of Numbers 23:1–30, we have
seen the powerful hands of almighty God protecting His people from
the wickedness of witchcraft. Israel was clothed in the beautiful spirit
of obedience unto God, and Balaam's evil plans and curses from his
twenty-one evil altars could not find any legal grounds on which to
land and take effect.

The very same can and had happened to people in our generation who study the Scriptures and make it applicable to their lives, in
walking in total obedience to God. It was and still is God who turn
the curses of the enemies into blessings for our good. If I had not
been a victim of evil altars and witchcraft, I would not have had an
experience and a story to share with you. It was my experience and
victorious deliverance from the spirit of witchcraft that allowed me
to totally give God the wheel of my life so that He can use me for
His great glory.

Witchcraft and its operation were very much alive and popular
in the land of Egypt, especially in Pharaoh's palace, according to the
book of Exodus. Pharoah, a grandmaster of witchcraft, used this evil
power to manipulate, control, and kill the lives and destinies of many
of God's people due to their ignorance and disobedience to God's
divine will.

*And Moses and Aaron went in unto Pharaoh,
and they did so as the Lord had commanded: and
Aaron cast down his rod before Pharaoh, and before
his servants, and it became a serpent. Then Pharaoh
also called the wise men and the sorcerers: now the
magicians of Egypt, they also did in like manner
with their enchantments. For they cast down every
man his rod, and they became serpents: but Aaron's*

rod swallowed up their rods. And the magicians of Egypt did so with their enchantments: and Pharaoh's heart was hardened, neither did he hearken unto them; as the Lord had said. (Exodus 7:10–12, 22)

The land of Canaan was no exception. But let us not forget that it is God who has the power over good and evil, according to the law of Isaiah 45:7. "I form the light, and create darkness: I make peace, and create evil: I the Lord do all these things."

Power belongs to our God. Satan and his kingdom must rely on the power of God, but Satan uses it to frame a law by mischief and not for the purpose of good because there is absolutely no good in him (see Psalm 94:20). It is beyond impossibility for Satan to do good; his nature is pure evil and wickedness (see John 8:44). However, the Lord God almighty has already sanctioned the spiritual law of destruction upon all the enemies that are using witchcraft against your life and destiny. Therefore, you can break free from the shackles of witchcraft, if you know how to fast and pray the correct way in the name of Jesus.

The law of Isaiah 58 is a powerful spiritual law that opens our spiritual eyes to the beautiful principles of a genuine fast. It is in line with the spiritual law of Matthew 17:21. "Howbeit this kind goeth not out but by prayer and fasting." However, demons and devils will not leave a person's life if he is going against spiritual principles, such as what was happening in verses 3 to 5 of Isaiah 58.

Wherefore have we fasted, say they and thou seest not? wherefore have we afflicted our soul, and thou takest no knowledge? Behold, in the day of your fast ye find pleasure, and exact all your labours. Behold, ye fast for strife and debate, and to smite with the fist of wickedness: ye shall not fast as ye do this day, to make your voice to be heard on high. (Isaiah 58:3–4)

A disobedient lifestyle, especially while on a fast, will activate the law of Deuteronomy 32:17: "They sacrificed unto devils, not to God; to gods whom they knew not, to new gods that came newly up, whom your fathers feared not."

It is no wonder the Lord God almighty commands Isaiah to cry out and lift up his voice like a trumpet and show the rebellious, who claim to be fasting unto God, their great transgressions. God wanted them to know that such fasting cannot be acknowledged by Him. Therefore, in verses 6 to 7 of Isaiah 58, God gave the outline of a genuine fast. This fast is considered as the genuine fast because it is designed by God to scatter any evil altar, break chains of bewitchment, destroy the spirit of witchcraft, and set any captive free in Jesus' name.

> *Is not this the fast that I have chosen? to loose the bands of wickedness, to undo the heavy burdens, and to let the oppressed go free, and that ye break every yoke? Is it not to deal thy bread to the hungry, and that thou bring the poor that are cast out to thy house? when thou seest the naked, that thou cover him; and that thou hide not thyself from thine own flesh?* (Isaiah 58:6–7)

This spiritual guide still stands even to this day and will continue to be a powerful warfare weapon against evil altars and witchcraft. God's Word is from everlasting to everlasting. Demons, devils, man, nor time cannot erase, change, or alter God's voice or His powerful words.

God is not partial. He always tells us what will happen to anyone who will dare to walk in obedience to His commandments, likewise what will happen if we choose to do the opposite. Hence, in verses 8 to 12 of Isaiah 58, He tells us exactly the reward of a genuine fast coupled with an obedient lifestyle.

> *Then shall thy light break forth as the morning, and thine health shall spring forth speedily:*

and thy righteousness shall go before thee; the glory of the LORD shall be thy reward. Then shalt thou call, and the LORD shall answer; thou shalt cry, and he shall say, Here I am. If thou take away from the midst of thee the yoke, the putting forth of the finger, and speaking vanity; And if thou draw out thy soul to the hungry, and satisfy the afflicted soul; then shall thy light rise in obscurity, and thy darkness be as the noon day: And the LORD shall guide thee continually, and satisfy thy soul in drought, and make fat thy bones: and thou shalt be like a watered garden, and like a spring of water, whose waters fail not. And they that shall be of thee shall build the old waste places: thou shalt raise up the foundations of many generations; and thou shalt be called, The repairer of the breach, The restorer of paths to dwell in. (Isaiah 58:8–12)

I cannot overlook the powerful law of Isaiah 58 verse 7 because now we can see that fasting will restore our health in a mighty and powerful way when it is done in God's prescribed way.

The truth is, that spiritual fasting and prayer are weapons against all forms of oppression. The fast should and will do the following for anyone who will follow the divine principles as it is God's prescription to get out what the Bible in Matthew 17 calls "this kind":

1. A genuine fast will "loose" the bands of wickedness that are spiritually set against your health. More than 90 percent of sicknesses, diseases, or infirmities come from evil altars. Jesus the Christ demonstrated this powerful truth as He went about healing and casting out demons and devils out of people's lives. One such powerful example is the woman who was bound by the spirit of infirmity for eighteen years and could not help herself. And if you are a good reader of your Bibles, you will quickly agree with me that the enemy uses sickness in many of our lives, if not all, to bind, yoke,

and oppress people's lives as this is his evil mandate. But Jesus will always set the captives free as this is the reason He came to our world (see Luke 4:18).

2. A genuine fast will undo the heavy burdens that are spiritually programmed in the heavenlies and in our dreams by evil altars. The fast will also pull down all triangular powers that are speaking against your destiny and cancel all negative negotiations of your father's and mother's houses that are standing in the way of your breakthrough in the name of Jesus.

3. Likewise, it will break all the evil yokes that have been placed around our necks, choking many into untimely graves and eternal condemnation.

4. Finally, you will be totally free as the evil hands of the flesh-eating and blood-drinking oppressors will be dried up, and the shackles of witchcraft will be broken in Jesus' mighty name.

Many are fasting and praying, but they have yet to implement these spiritual principles in their fasting and prayer lives. And like the Israelites at the time who were fasting for strife and wickedness, God cannot hear neither answer such fast. He will not answer until we change the way we approach fasting and prayers. God will not answer our cries until we are living our lives in His ordained way.

It is obvious that there is only one way to be set free from the evil spirit of witchcraft, and it is not by fighting evil with evil but by a life of obedience to divine authority and genuine fasting and prayer. However, one must also seek to maintain his deliverance by regular studying of the Scriptures. It is a fact according to the law of Matthew 12:43–45 that once an unclean spirit is cast out of a man, he should stay out because once he regains entrance back into the person's life, that person will be in greater danger. The sickness, disease, financial problems, or whatever else that was wreaking havoc in the person's life will be of a greater challenge than before.

When the unclean spirit is gone out of a man,
he walketh through dry places, seeking rest, and fin-

deth none. Then he saith, I will return into my house from whence I came out; and when he is come, he findeth it empty, swept, and garnished. Then goeth he, and taketh with himself seven other spirits more wicked than himself, and they enter in and dwell there: and the last state of that man is worse than the first. Even so shall it be also unto this wicked generation. (Matthew 12:43–45)

Now having engaged in the genuine fasting and prayer as outlined in the law of Isaiah 58, immediately, my sleep pattern improved the very first night of the fast. And by the end of that three-day dry fast, I was getting at least three hours of sleep each night.

I was excited because the Word of God did exactly what it promised! It defeated principalities and powers out of my life and set me totally free.

I went on several fasting and prayer sessions. And I became a lover and a doer of God's Words, according to the law of James 1. "But be ye doers of the word, and not hearers only, deceiving your own selves" (James 1:22). I, therefore, made a promise to God that if He would heal me and set me free, I would follow Him all the way as I give my life totally for His service.

I am happy to tell you that God did just that. The Lord then led me to minister in writing daily devotionals.

The Holy Spirit then spoke to me to put all my writings into books so that the world can have access to them. Because many who have read the devotionals that the Holy Spirit allowed me to share each morning have seen breakthroughs in all areas or departments of their lives, especially their health.

And now I want to share the same principles that had and continue to set me, my family, and those to whom I minister free from the shackles of witchcraft in the powerful name of Jesus the Christ. Now that I am free from the shackles of witchcraft, the Spirit of the Lord is upon me. He has anointed me to preach deliverance messages of freedom to the captives and to proclaim liberty to all those who have been bound by this evil and wicked principality known as witchcraft in the powerful name of Jesus the Christ.

CHAPTER 2

Quenching the Fiery Darts of the Enemy

Above all, taking the shield of faith, wherewith ye shall be able to quench all the fiery darts of the wicked.

—Ephesians 6:16

The apostle Paul, writing unto the believers at Ephesus in Ephesians 6:16, admonished and told them in his epistle: "Above all, taking the shield of faith, wherewith ye shall be able to quench all the fiery darts of the wicked."

But before we can understand what exactly the apostle Paul means by "the shield of faith," we must first seek an understanding of what the word *faith* means because we are told that it is faith that stops these satanic fiery darts from prospering in our lives.

Therefore, what is faith, according to the Scriptures?

The law of Hebrews 11 gives the most powerful definition for the word *faith*. However, if our spiritual eyes are still not open to spiritual things, we will be unable to walk away with the correct understanding of this powerful spiritual warfare weapon known as faith.

Now faith is the substance of things hoped for, the evidence of things not seen. (Hebrews 11:1)

So faith in a nutshell is a spirit from God's kingdom, given to us as a gift through the powerful Word of God. However, applying the Word to our lives activates faith (*or puts faith to work*) so that the manifestation(s) can be seen in the physical of our lives. The Bible is clear in Romans chapter 12 that everyone (*Christian and non-Christian alike*) is given a measure of faith by God.

This means that all of us have the legal right through the Word of God, who is Jesus the Christ, to be saved and be set free when we activate the Word.

> *For I say to every man that is among you, through the grace given unto me, not to think of himself more highly than he ought to think, but to think soberly according as God hath dealt to every man the measure of faith.* (Romans 12:3)

It is in the law of Ephesians 2 that we really understand how important and serious this spirit of faith is. Because without faith, none of us can be saved in God's eternal kingdom, as stated by the Word of God, "For by grace are ye saved through faith; and that not of yourselves: it is the gift of God: Not of works, lest any man should boast" (Ephesians 2:8–9).

But again, the choice will be ours as God forces no one!

Therefore, we will all agree that what the apostle is saying is that we should use the Word of God to combat the lies and the works of darkness in the name of Jesus. And just to give a heads-up on what Satan's fiery darts are, we will look carefully at the law of John 10:10a: "The thief cometh not, but for to steal, and to kill, and to destroy." The darts are anything that come into our lives to kill, steal, and destroy us. And that is exactly what the spirit of witchcraft does to a person's life.

But without faith, it is impossible to be victorious over the enemy's darts. The apostle helps us to understand that it is the shield of faith that quenches the fiery darts that are fired against us. I am super excited that it is God who has given us the weapon of our warfare to fight the enemy of our souls, as is written in 2 Corinthians 10:4, "For the weapons of our warfare are not carnal, but mighty through God to the pulling down of stronghold."

And as Christians, we have absolutely no reason to be overpowered by the wickedness that is coming from the kingdom of darkness, regardless of the evil vessels that Satan chooses to use. The aforementioned text is a very serious and powerful spiritual warfare law that comes to set the captives free if used in the spirit of faith and obedience to the principles of God.

Satan, the enemy of our souls, is currently firing fiery darts at us: darts of witchcraft, sicknesses and diseases, confusion and chaos, poverty, divorce, immorality, and hardship, the list continues. But with the powerful shield of faith, you and I can and must put a stop to these evil fiery darts in the mighty name of Jesus the Christ.

However, it is important to note that the Christian's life is a life of spiritual warfare; and we must fight the good fight of faith as declared in 1 Timothy 6:12b, "Fight the good of faith." But there are different strategies of warfare as seen in 2 Chronicles 20:22, "And when they began to sing and praise, the LORD set ambushments against the children of Ammon, Moab, and Mount Se-ir." So here we discover that praise is a mighty weapon in the hands of the believers against Satan's fiery darts. Satan's weapon against us is his fiery darts. But one of the Christians' weapons is that of praising God, regardless of the fiery darts that are coming at us.

Satan will send these darts at everyone, especially the ignorant. But what will make the difference whether these darts prosper in our lives or not is the spiritual application of knowledge of how to use the shield of faith as a weapon. Therefore, it must be noted that faith is also a mighty warfare weapon that causes all the other spiritual weapons to be effective. Satanic fiery darts are so many, that it will be impossible to list all of them. But any evil thing that stands in the way of your eternal and divine destiny is considered to be satanic fiery darts. Evil altars and the power of witchcraft are the most common fiery darts that the enemy uses to hijack people's divine greatness. Nonetheless, do not be alarmed because for every dart that the enemy will fire at us, there is also a spiritual weapon to combat it.

The Bible is clear in the law of Matthew 17:21 that certain kinds of darts will not come out except through fasting and prayers. Hence, here we see that fasting and prayer is another powerful weapon to put a stop to satanic fiery darts in the all-powerful name of Jesus the Christ. However, spiritual ignorance of the laws of God causes many to experience Satan's fiery darts, and I was one such person before I activated the power of Proverbs 11:9b and received deliverance in the name of Jesus. It is Isaiah 5:13 that tells us that God's people have gone into captivity because they lack knowledge, and Hosea 4:6 reinforces it. Hence, you will agree with me that the spirit of ignorance is a major doorway opener in the lives of many Christians, which hinders the warfare weapons from working against Satanic fiery darts. When we look at the law of Ephesians 6, it is also a clear indication that we should have already been dressed in the armor of the Lord before Satan's fiery darts came up against us.

Satan knows that if we are not dressed for spiritual battles, then eventually his darts will manifest in our physical lives. It is a spiritual fact that God has all the powers over good and evil, and He has already destroyed Satan and his fiery darts by His death, burial, and triumphant resurrection from the grave and has given us the power to do the same (see Luke 10:19).

Our lives must be pleasing to God before He can destroy our enemies. And again, in order to please God, we must have the spirit of faith according to Hebrews 11:6, "But without faith, it is impossible to please Him: for he that cometh to God must believe that He is and that He is a rewarder of them that diligently seek him."

When we look at how the devil's fiery darts are sending thousands of Christians to untimely graves, we can conclude that there are many faithless Christians in our churches. Their lives are not pleasing to God, so they are at the mercy of the enemy. It makes absolutely no sense to be in buildings called churches, singing, praying, and reading the Bible, and when it is time for the shield of faith to be lifted up against the devil, the spirits of doubt and fear hold back your hands. I know that many Christians do not talk about the Holy Ghost and Holy Ghost fire, but if you are not baptized with the Holy Spirit and fire, you will not understand the principles of spiritual warfare. And neither are you winning against these fiery darts that Satan is firing at you and your family. See Acts 1:8, "But ye shall receive power, after that the Holy Ghost is come upon you: and ye shall be witnesses unto me both in Jerusalem, and in all Judaea, and in Samaria, and unto the uttermost part of the earth."

Years ago, the enemies, Satan, and his agents were firing their fiery darts of witchcraft at me, robbing me of my health and happiness. The enemies tried to do me just as Jezebel the witch did to Naboth the ignorant in the spirit with her evil witchcraft altars as explained in 1 Kings 21:1–14:

> And it came to pass after these things, that Naboth the Jezreelite had a vineyard, which was in Jezreel, hard by the palace of Ahab king of Samaria. And Ahab spake unto Naboth, saying, Give me thy vineyard, that I may have it for a garden of herbs, because it is near unto my house: and I will give thee for it a better vineyard than it; or, if it seem good to thee, I will give thee the worth of it in money. And Naboth said to Ahab, The LORD forbid it me, that I should give the inheritance of my fathers unto thee. And Ahab came into his house heavy and displeased because of the word which Naboth the Jezreelite had spoken to him: for he had said, I will not give thee the inheritance of my fathers. And he laid him down upon his bed, and turned away his face, and would eat no bread. But Jezebel his wife came to him, and said unto him, Why is thy spirit so sad, that thou eatest no bread? And he said unto her, Because I spake unto Naboth the Jezreelite, and said unto him, Give me thy vineyard for money; or else, if it please thee, I will give thee another vineyard for it: and he answered, I will not give thee my vineyard. And Jezebel his wife said unto him, Dost thou now govern the kingdom of Israel? arise, and eat

bread, and let thine heart be merry: I will give thee the vineyard of Naboth the Jezreelite. So she wrote letters in Ahab's name, and sealed them with his seal, and sent the letters unto the elders and to the nobles that were in his city, dwelling with Naboth. And she wrote in the letters, saying, Proclaim a fast, and set Naboth on high among the people: And set two men, sons of Belial, before him, to bear witness against him, saying, Thou didst blaspheme God and the king. And then carry him out, and stone him, that he may die. And the men of his city, even the elders and the nobles who were the inhabitants in his city, did as Jezebel had sent unto them, and as it was written in the letters which she had sent unto them. They proclaimed a fast, and set Naboth on high among the people. And there came in two men, children of Belial, and sat before him: and the men of Belial witnessed against him, even against Naboth, in the presence of the people, saying, Naboth did blaspheme God and the king. Then they carried him forth out of the city, and stoned him with stones, that he died. Then they sent to Jezebel, saying, Naboth is stoned, and is dead.

But when the spirit of knowledge came, power had also shifted hands, and I started gaining victory over principalities and powers in the name of Jesus the Christ. I know that like myself, when you have had enough, you will begin to engage yourself in powerful spiritual warfare fights against the enemy, using the sword of the Spirit, which is the Word of God, and you too, will become victorious over all his fiery darts in your life and the lives of your loved ones.

Having understood the spiritual principles, you will not even wait for the enemies to come to you because you will be so bold and confident in the Word of God that you will now take the war to the enemies' gates to disarm them with the law of Luke 10:19. "Behold,

I give unto you the power to tread on serpents and scorpions, and over all the power of the enemy: and nothing shall by any means hurt you."

Reference no. 2: "And having disarmed the powers and authorities, He made a public spectacle of them, triumphing over them by the cross" (Colossians 2:15 NIV). "He disarmed the rulers and authorities and put them to open shame, by triumphing over them in him" (Colossians 2:15 ESV).

Remember, as Christians, we are more than conquerors through Christ. "Nay, in all these things we are more than conquerors through him that loved us" (Romans 8:37). I know already that great things are awaiting all those who would now follow the divine principles of the Scriptures. Because it takes faith to really please the Lord and break the shackles of witchcraft that are strangulating your relationship with God, your lives, your homes, your marriages, your families, and your entire bloodline.

CHAPTER 3

Humbling Ourselves for Deliverance

Seest thou how Ahab humbleth himself before me? Because he humbleth himself before me, I will not bring the evil in his days.

—1 Kings 21:29

The Lord is reminding you of His amazing power. He is telling you that there is hope. There is hope in turning your situation(s) or problem(s) around, hope for the recovery of your health and happiness, financial hope, hope and freedom of eternal salvation in God.

Here is the truth: no matter how hopeless or worthless your situation might appear in this physical world, in the spirit, where our God of the impossibilities resides, there is hope if our hearts remain humble.

The Bible speaks clearly in the following scriptures about the presence of God with the humble. God cannot live in anyone who refuses to be humble. And humility starts with us loving and living by the Word of God. God will give grace and show compassion to all those who are humble as outlined in James 4:6: "But he giveth more grace. Wherefore he saith, God resisteth the proud, but giveth grace unto the humble."

Humility is the key that opens the powerful hands of God unto us. When one is humble, he is also obedient to divine principles as a rebellious person does not have the spirit of humility. And God is far from such a life as He only dwells and abides with the humble.

> *For thus saith the high and lofty One that inhabiteth eternity, whose name is Holy; I dwell in the high and holy place, with him also that is of a contrite and humble spirit, to revive the spirit of the humble, and to revive the heart of the contrite ones.* (Isaiah 57:15)

Catch this! God will resist you if your heart is highly lifted up; you must remain humble to see the power of God in your life.

> *Though the Lord be high, yet hath he respect unto the lowly: but the proud he knoweth afar off.* (Psalm 138:6)

Let us be reminded that God is able to answer our cries if we genuinely seek His face out of humble hearts.

> *Because, thine heart was tender, and thou didst humble thyself before God, when thou heardest his words against this place, and against the inhabitants thereof, and humblest thyself before me, and didst rend thy clothes, and weep before me; I have even heard thee also, saith the Lord.* (2 Chronicles 34:27)

A humble heart will attract the deliverance power of God in defeating the powers of darkness that are attacking your lives. There are absolutely no limitations with God! However, God will not work in our favor if we refuse to love Him and do His commandments.

Therefore, the first step in solving your problems or situation is for you to first choose who you want to be the master of your life according to the law of Joshua 24.

It is God who gave man the freedom of choice as choices will be the first significant step in determining our victory or our defeat, depending on whom we choose to serve and obey. "Choose ye this day whom you will serve" (Joshua 24:15).

One thing is for sure, Jesus the Christ, He has never lost a battle, and He never will as can clearly be seen in the story of Jehoshaphat in 2 Chronicles 20 below.

> *And they rose early in the morning, and went forth into the wilderness of Tekoa: and as they went forth, Jehoshaphat stood and said, Hear me, O Judah, and ye inhabitants of Jerusalem; Believe in the Lord your God, so shall ye be established; believe his prophets, so shall ye prosper.*
>
> *And when he had consulted with the people, he appointed singers unto the Lord, and that should praise the beauty of holiness, as they went out before the army, and to say, Praise the Lord; for his mercy endureth for ever.*
>
> *And when they began to sing and to praise, the Lord set ambushments against the children of Ammon, Moab, and mount Seir, which were come against Judah; and they were smitten.*
>
> *For the children of Ammon and Moab stood up against the inhabitants of mount Seir, utterly to slay and destroy them: and when they had made an end of the inhabitants of Seir, every one helped to destroy another.*
>
> *And when Judah came toward the watch tower in the wilderness, they looked unto the multitude, and, behold, they were dead bodies fallen to the earth, and none escaped.*

> *And when Jehoshaphat and his people came to take away the spoil of them, they found among them in abundance both riches with the dead bodies, and precious jewels, which they stripped off for themselves, more than they could carry away: and they were three days in gathering of the spoil, it was so much.* (2 Chronicles 20:20–25)

Indeed the Lord is a man of war!

God will only fight for us if and when we choose Him. Because even though He is God and He can do all things, He, too, must respect His own rules, in allowing us to choose. When we read through the book of 1 Kings, we realize that Ahab's lifestyle was in total opposition to the laws of God. The truth is, Ahab was a wicked king who had also married a wicked witch, known as Jezebel. See 2 Kings 9:22b.

The amount of evil that both Ahab and Jezebel had committed before the Lord would outnumber all the evil that you and I could possibly do in our lifetime. Wickedness was a way of life for both of them. But the God of heaven was ready to forgive Ahab and even withdrew the punishment until later after his death because he humbled himself. However, the sons of Ahab did receive a spiritual transfusion of the bloodline curses from all the wickedness he, Ahab, had done as can be seen in the story of 2 Kings 9.

> And thou shalt smite the house of Ahab thy master, that I may avenge the blood of my servants the prophets, and the blood of all the servants of the Lord, at the hand of Jezebel. For the whole house of Ahab shall perish: and I will cut off from Ahab him that pisseth against the wall, and him that is shut up and left in Israel: And I will make the house of Ahab like the house of Jeroboam the son of Nebat, and like the house of Baasha the son of Ahijah: And the dogs shall eat

Jezebel in the portion of Jezreel, and there shall
be none to bury her. And he opened the door,
and fled. (2 Kings 9:7–10).

Ahab's punishment would later serve as a generational curse!
"Our fathers have sinned, and are not; and we have borne their iniquities" (Lamentations 5:7). Ahab was forgiven because he made a
choice to choose God (at the time), and he thereby humbled himself and escaped the punishment. However, all of Ahab's family had
inherited his curses. And this bloodline curse caused his seventy sons
to be killed as can be seen in the story here in 2 Kings 10.

And Ahab had seventy sons in Samaria. And
Jehu wrote letters, and sent to Samaria, unto the
rulers of Jezreel, to the elders, and to them that
brought up Ahab's children, saying, Now as soon
as this letter cometh to you, seeing your master's
sons are with you, and there are with you chariots
and horses, a fenced city also, and armour; look
even out the best and meetest of your master's
sons, and set him on his father's throne, and fight
for your master's house. But they were exceed-
ingly afraid, and said, Behold, two kings stood
not before him: how then shall we stand? And
he that was over the house, and he that was over
the city, the elders also, and the bringers up of
the children, sent to Jehu, saying, We are thy servants, and will do all that thou shalt bid us; we
will not make any king: do thou that which is
good in thine eyes. Then he wrote a letter the
second time to them, saying, If ye be mine, and if
ye will hearken unto my voice, take ye the heads
of the men your master's sons, and come to me
to Jezreel by tomorrow this time. Now the king's
sons, being seventy persons, were with the great
men of the city, which brought them up. And it

28

came to pass, when the letter came to them, that they took the king's sons, and slew seventy persons, and put their heads in baskets, and sent him them to Jezreel. And there came a messenger, and told him, saying, They have brought the heads of the king's sons. And he said, Lay ye them in two heaps at the entering in of the gate until the morning. And it came to pass in the morning, that he went out, and stood, and said to all the people, Ye be righteous: behold, I conspired against my master, and slew him: but who slew all these? Know now that there shall fall unto the earth nothing of the word of the LORD, which the LORD spake concerning the house of Ahab: for the LORD hath done that which he spake by his servant Elijah. So Jehu slew all that remained of the house of Ahab in Jezreel, and all his great men, and his kinsfolks, and his priests, until he left him none remaining. (2 Kings 10:1–11)

It is imperative for us to understand that God is not partial. "Then Peter opened his mouth, and said, Of a truth, I perceive that God is no respecter of persons" (Acts 10:34). Therefore, if God could have pardoned Ahab's sins and spared him, how much more will He do for you and me when we choose Him? God will and can fight all your battles of impossibilities when you choose to be on His team. According to Deuteronomy 3:22, "Ye shall not fear them: for the Lord your God he shall fight for you," indeed, "He is a man of war."

God is not only a man of war, but He is a healer and a restorer of our health. The story of Hezekiah proves the fact that God can and will heal our bodies, and just like Hezekiah, He will add more length of days to our lives if we cry out to Him and seek His face.

Second Kings 20:1–6 reads:

> *In those days was Hezekiah sick unto death. And the prophet Isaiah the son of Amoz came to*

him, and said unto him, Thus saith the Lord, Set thine house in order; for thou shalt die, and not live.

Then he turned his face to the wall, and prayed unto the Lord, saying,

I beseech thee, O Lord, remember now how I have walked before thee in truth and with a perfect heart, and have done that which is good in thy sight. And Hezekiah wept sore.

And it came to pass, afore Isaiah was gone out into the middle court, that the word of the Lord came to him, saying,

Turn again, and tell Hezekiah the captain of my people, Thus saith the Lord, the God of David thy father, I have heard thy prayer, I have seen thy tears: behold, I will heal thee: on the third day thou shalt go up unto the house of the Lord.

And I will add unto thy days fifteen years; and I will deliver thee and this city out of the hand of the king of Assyria; I will defend this city for mine own sake, and for my servant David's sake.

It is therefore important for us to know that whenever God looks at us, He looks at us from our hearts or minds like Hezekiah's. And healing will only occur in our bodies if our hearts or minds are pleasing to God.

But the Lord said unto Samuel, Look not on his countenance, or on the height of his stature; because I have refused him: for the Lord seeth not as man seeth; for man looketh on the outward appearance, but the Lord looketh on the heart. (1 Samuel 16:7)

So the questions I want to ask you in this chapter are, how is it with your heart? Is it humble? Because a humble heart is one that wants to genuinely please God. It is a heart that is governed by the beautiful spirit of obedience to His words. It is a heart that is sorry for all the evil and wickedness that one has done.

It is a repentant heart that seeks to take on the mind of Jesus the Christ.

> The sacrifices of God are a broken spirit: a broken and a contrite heart, O God, thou wilt not despise. (Psalm 51:17)

God wants to heal you and extend your life with health and happiness. He wants to bless you in all departments of your life. Friends, God wants you to live in the land of blessings. He also wants you to prosper and be in good health while you continue to humble yourself and walk in obedience to all of His commandments according to the beautiful law of Deuteronomy 28.

> *Blessed shalt thou be in the city, and blessed shalt thou be in the field.*
>
> *Blessed shall be the fruit of thy body, and the fruit of thy ground, and the fruit of thy cattle, the increase of thy kine, and the flocks of thy sheep.*
>
> *Blessed shall be thy basket and thy store.*
>
> *Blessed shalt thou be when thou comest in, and blessed shalt thou be when thou goest out.*
>
> *The Lord shall cause thine enemies that rise up against thee to be smitten before thy face: they shall come out against thee one way, and flee before thee seven ways.*
>
> *The Lord shall command the blessing upon thee in thy storehouses, and in all that thou settest thine hand unto; and he shall bless thee in the land which the Lord thy God giveth thee.*
>
> *The Lord shall establish thee an holy people unto himself, as he hath sworn unto thee if thou shalt keep the commandments of the Lord thy God, and walk in his ways.*

And all people of the earth shall see that thou art called by the name of the Lord; and they shall be afraid of thee.

And the Lord shall make thee plenteous in goods, in the fruit of thy body, and in the fruit of thy cattle, and in the fruit of thy ground, in the land which the Lord sware unto thy fathers to give thee.

The Lord shall open unto thee his good treasure, the heaven to give the rain unto thy land in his season, and to bless all the work of thine hand: and thou shalt lend unto many nations, and thou shalt not borrow.

And the Lord shall make thee the head, and not the tail; and thou shalt be above only, and thou shalt not be beneath; if that thou hearken unto the commandments of the Lord thy God, which I command thee this day, to observe and to do them:

And thou shalt not go aside from any of the words which I command thee this day, to the right hand, or to the left, to go after other gods to serve them. (Deuteronomy 28:3–14)

God is a reciprocal God! And He wants relationships with us! It is a spiritual fact that God is waiting on you right now to turn over that problem to Him. He is standing ready to fight all your battles. The truth is all of your battles belong to God.

Thus saith the Lord unto you, Be not afraid nor dismayed by reason of this great multitude; for the battle is not yours, but God's. (2 Chronicles 20:15b)

But the questions are, like Hezekiah, will you let Him? Will you let God heal you and multiply the years of your life? Will you let Him into the secret parts of your life, that department that no one seems to understand? Yes! I know you have told everyone that you are doing well. But you also know that you are hurting way down inside your heart from the effects of witchcraft.

You are worried about that doctor's report.

You are worried about those bills.

You are worried about that divorce.

You are worried about the children.

You are worried about running out of time and the like.

But the power is actually in your hands because when you activate the law of Joshua 24:15 and choose to do life God's way, the enemy will have to release you as power shifts hands and the evil wall altars of the enemies will be pulled down.

The power of choice is still yours; what are you waiting on?

CHAPTER 4

Pulling Down the Evil Wall Altars of the Enemies

The Lord said unto Joshua, see, I have given into thine hand Jericho, the king thereof, and the mighty men of valour.

—Joshua 6:2

There is a good reason I entitled this chapter "Pulling Down the Evil Wall Altars of the Enemies." God is sending you the spiritual tools you will need, in this chapter, to pull down the walls of idolatry and the evil foundations of your father's and mother's houses. He is showing you how to be set free from wicked powers and evil principalities in the powerful name of Jesus the Christ.

It is Jesus who exposes the fact that only by the truth can one really be set free! "And ye shall know the truth, and the truth shall make you free" (John 8:32).

God wants you to experience freedom and deliverance in all departments of your life!

But first, like Joshua, we need to hear the voice of the Lord telling us that He has already given us the permission to pull down our Jericho walls in the name of Jesus. And the law of John 8 reassures us that God has indeed given us the right to move in and tear down these evil walls that are spiritually set up against our divine destinies.

"If the Son, therefore, shall make you free, ye shall be free indeed" (John 8:38).

Now that we have God's approval, like Joshua, we need to know the types of tools to use in getting the job done. Because, even though the walls look like they are physical, the truth is they are rather spiritual or invisible walls with great demonic forces behind them.

It is a spiritual fact that our battles are rather spiritual, and at no point in time should a true child of God engage in any physical fights with anyone, according to the law of 2 Corinthians 10, "For though we walk in the flesh, we do not war after the flesh. For the weapons of our warfare are not carnal but mighty through God to the pulling down of strongholds. Casting down imaginations and every high thing that exalteth itself against the knowledge of God and bringing into captivity every thought to the obedience of Christ" (2 Corinthians 10:3–5).

Therefore, we need prayer, as a spiritual invisible tool like Jehoshaphat, as seen here below in the narrative of 2 Chronicles 20:

> And Jehoshaphat feared, and set himself to seek the Lord, and proclaimed a fast throughout all Judah. And Judah gathered themselves together, to ask helped of the Lord: even out of all the cities of Judah they came to seek the Lord. And Jehoshaphat stood in the congregation of Judah and Jerusalem, in the house of the Lord, before the new court, And said, O Lord God of our fathers, art not thou God in heaven? and rulest not thou over all the kingdoms of the heathen? and in thine hand is there not power and might, so that none is able to withstand thee? Art not thou our God, who didst drive out the inhabitants of this land before thy people Israel, and gavest it to the seed of Abraham thy friend for ever? And they dwelt therein, and have built thee a sanctuary therein for thy name, saying, If, when evil cometh upon us, as the sword, judgment, or pestilence, or famine, we stand before this house, and in

*thy presence, (for thy name is in this house,) and cry
unto thee in our affliction, then thou wilt hear and
help.* (2 Chronicles 20:3–9)

More so, we need the proper attire; we need to put on the full armour of the Lord as we seek to march around these evil wall altars using God's special number, seven, to bring total destruction to these evil altars in the powerful name of Jesus the Christ. "Put on the whole armour of God, that ye may be able to stand against the wiles of the devil" (Ephesians 6:11). Now as a child of God, in your battles against the kingdom of darkness, you will always win if you stay on the Lord's side, avoid distractions, and live above sin.

The law of Joshua 6:2 is divine proof that God had already given into our hands the heads of our enemies. And He is waiting for us to now go in and destroy them by pulling down their evil altars using the powerful sword of the Spirit—the Word of God—and the blood of Jesus the Christ. It is important to understand that when God gives a promise to His people, He keeps it, and He is expecting us to move in with faith and accomplish the task.

It is necessary for us to understand that the Word of the Lord is God's voice and it is extremely powerful. It is therefore the only Word that can speak to both the visible and the invisible realms at the same time with supernatural power that no other powers can contradict, overthrow, or deny. It is sharp and quick. It fights against evil and its works, including demons and devils, in the name of Jesus. It cuts bad habits. It heals and delivers, and most importantly, it will and has set captives free if they walk in the spirit of divine obedience to the Word.

"For the word of God is quick, and powerful, and sharper than any two-edged sword, piercing even to the dividing asunder of soul and spirit, and of the joints and marrow, and is a discerner of the thoughts and intents of the heart" (Hebrews 4:12).

The Bible is clear! We must cut down the evil altars of our enemies and burn their groves, using the Holy Ghost fire and the hammer of the Lord to scatter and destroy all the evil works of the enemies, according to the law of Deuteronomy 12.

> *And ye shall overthrow their altars, and break*
> *their pillars, and burn their groves with fire; and*
> *ye shall hew down the graven images of their gods,*
> *and destroy the names of them out of that place.*
> (Deuteronomy 12:3)

God used a Gideon to show us a pictural view of how to perform spiritual guerilla warfare against an evil altar. Such warfare will destroy all that the enemies have set up against you and your family. With such guerilla warfare, you will begin to trample upon the spiritual serpents and scorpions and over all the evil works of the devil, and nothing shall by any means hurt you in the victorious name of Jesus as seen in the text below.

> Then Gideon took ten men of his servants,
> and did as the LORD had said unto him: and so
> it was, because he feared his father's household,
> and the men of the city, that he could not do it by
> day, that he did it by night. And when the men
> of the city arose early in the morning, behold, the
> altar of Baal was cast down, and the grove was cut
> down that was by it, and the second bullock was
> offered upon the altar that was built. And they
> said one to another, Who hath done this thing?
> And when they enquired and asked, they said,
> Gideon the son of Joash hath done this thing.
> (Judges 6:27–29)

There is a specific way and specific criteria to use the weapons of God in destroying the enemies and their evil walls or altars. The truth is, if there are active sins in our lives, we will not be able to use the weapons of God to defeat the enemies, as Satan cannot cast out Satan. "And if Satan cast out Satan, he is divided against himself; how shall then his kingdom stand?" (Matthew 12:26). Likewise, the evil walls or altars cannot be destroyed if there are iniquities in our hearts, as stated by the law of Psalm 66, "If I regard iniquity in my heart, the Lord will not hear me" (Psalm 66:18).

In order for us to be victorious in this warfare, we need to have faith in God, like Gideon or Joshua, as it will be our first weapon in pulling down any evil walls or altars. You must possess unflinching faith in God. A doubter is a sinner, and a sinner cannot receive the promises meant for the righteous.

> *But let him ask in faith, nothing wavering.*
> *For he that wavereth is like a wave of the sea driven*
> *with the wind and tossed. For let not that man*
> *think that he shall receive any thing of the Lord.*
> *A double-minded man is unstable in all his ways.*
> (James 1:6–8)

As we reflect again on Joshua 6:2, we will quickly understand that God was speaking to Joshua about a job that had already been done in the Spirit. However, Joshua had to have unshifting faith in the word that God has spoken in order to see the manifestation of it in the physical. Why? Because God's words are spirit and they are life as declared in the law of John 6, "The words that I speak unto you, they are spirit, and they are life" (John 6:63).

Let us go deeper as we seek to understand the power of our first weapon, faith, because it is what will allow all the other powerful divine weapons to be activated in destroying those evil, Jericho, witchcraft walls that are standing against our divine destinies of greatness, in the name of Jesus Christ. It was by faith that all the disciples, the patriarchs, prophets, and the great men and women of God, including me, slayed their Goliaths and drowned their Pharaohs.

See Bible reference Ephesians 11:1–9:

> *Now faith is the substance of things hoped for,*
> *the evidence of things not seen. For by it the elders*
> *obtained a good report. Through faith we under-*
> *stand that the worlds were framed by the word of*
> *God, so that things which are seen were not made*

of things which do appear. By faith Abel offered unto God a more excellent sacrifice than Cain, by which he obtained witness that he was righteous, God testifying of his gifts: and by it he being dead yet speaketh. By faith Enoch was translated that he should not see death; and was not found, because God had translated him: for before his translation he had this testimony, that he pleased God. But without faith it is impossible to please him: for he that cometh to God must believe that he is, and that he is a rewarder of them that diligently seek him. By faith Noah, being warned of God of things not seen as yet, moved with fear, prepared an ark to the saving of his house; by the which he condemned the world, and became heir of the righteousness which is by faith. By faith Abraham, when he was called to go out into a place which he should after receive for an inheritance, obeyed; and he went out, not knowing whither he went. By faith he sojourned in the land of promise, as in a strange country, dwelling in tabernacles with Isaac and Jacob, the heirs with him of the same promise.

Yes! The weapon of faith is a lifetime victorious weapon that the righteous continues to use against the wiles of the enemies.

The Bible is clear; the walls of Jericho came down by the powerful weapon of faith and the spirit of obedience to the command of God.

> By faith, the walls of Jericho fell down, after they were compassed about seven days. (Hebrews 11:30)
>
> And Samuel said, Hath the Lord as great delight in burnt offerings and sacrifices, as in obeying the voice of the Lord? Behold, to obey is

better than sacrifice, and to hearken than the fat
of rams. (1 Samuel 15:22)

The laws of Hebrews chapter 11 and 1 Samuel chapter 15 boldly
outlined the two major spiritual weapons of breaking the shackles of
witchcraft permanently out of our lives. It is not until we are dressed
in the garment of faith and obedience to God and His Word that we
can and will break the shackles of witchcraft permanently from our
lives.

I am sure by now your spiritual eyes would have been opened
to the fact that you cannot tear down your Jericho walls without
faith and obedience to the voice of God. "And it shall come to pass,
if thou shalt hearken diligently unto the voice of the Lord thy God,
to observe and to do all his commandments which I command thee
this day, that the Lord thy God will set thee on high above all nations
of the earth: And all these blessings shall come on thee, and over-
take thee, if thou shalt hearken unto the voice of the Lord thy God"
(Deuteronomy 28:1-2). For far too long, many people are failing
at pulling down the evil altars that are speaking against their divine
destinies because they are using the wrong weapons.

On the other hand, many are failing at destroying their Jericho
walls of bloodline curses, evil foundations, family idols, evil negotiations that were made by parents, relatives, loved ones, and the like.
Because rather than tearing these evil altars down, they are empower-
ing them through the evil spirit of ignorance to spiritual principles.
As declared in the law of Hosea 4, "My people are destroyed for lack
of knowledge: because thou hast rejected knowledge, I will also reject
thee, that thou shalt be no priest to me: seeing thou hast forgotten
the law of thy God, I will also forget thy children" (Hosea 4:6).

If Joshua had refused to follow faithfully the divine instructions
of the Lord, then instead of the Jericho wall being destroyed, he,
Joshua, and the Israelites would have been destroyed. The very same
warning goes for all of us. It is full time for us to obey the rules of
God and break the shackles of witchcraft and be set free like faithful
Joshua, Jehoshaphat, and Gideon as seen in the various Bible stories
throughout this chapter.

Anyone who will not take heed to the instructions of God will lose the battle. Because as human beings, Christians and non-Christians alike, battles are all spiritual and need to be fought with the divine weapon of obedience to the commands of God. It is a fact that many people within our churches want to sow seeds (give monies) in order to get their healing, wealth, prosperity, and success.

They hate the idea of walking in obedience to God's principles. The evil spirit of pride is like a chain that has been placed around their stubborn necks, pulling them away from their divine breakthroughs. They hate to forgive, and they will not break company with the evil spirits of envy, jealousy, bitterness, gossip, hatred, hypocrisy, ritual, and tradition.

I know that you might be looking for some super tricks to scatter your Jericho walls, but the only weapon, according to the laws of God, is the weapon that Joshua uses: the warfare weapon of divine obedience to the commandments of God. God cannot work for you if you do not love Him and do all His commandments. "If you love me keep my commandments" (John 14:15).

CHAPTER 5

God's Angelic Protection

The angel of the Lord encampeth round about them that fear Him, and delivereth them. (Psalm 34:7)

God is sending us a powerful message from the above text. It is a word of assurance and protection for all those who will seek to understand the power of the text, especially during a spiritual warfare battle with the enemy.

So come on this journey with me as we search the Scriptures and find out if it is possible for God's angel to pitch their tents around us and the enemies of fear, doubts, hatred, unforgiveness, sickness, poverty, oppression, witchcraft, evil yokes, bondages, and the like to still have their evil hands in our lives, with the legal right to carry out their evil mandate as stated in John 10.

"The thief cometh not, but for to steal, and to kill, and to destroy" (John 10:10a). In addition, we want to look at what gives the enemy spiritual right, because according to the law of Proverbs 26, for the curses to operate in our lives, we must be breaking the commandments of God. "As the bird by wandering, as the swallow by flying, So the curse causeless shall not come" (Proverbs 26:2). No curse will come into a person's life if he is not going against divine authority or principles.

The rhetorical question of Hebrews 1:14 helps us to understand the roles of God's angels in the lives of the believers even though there is absolutely no instruction given to us by God wherein we must ask or pray to an angel to do anything for us or to encamp around us, as it is God who gives His angels the commands. Not man!

The first thing I want to draw our attention to is the word *fear*. Because in order for the angels of the Lord to dwell around us, we must fear the Lord. But what is this fear, and how do we activate it in our lives to have the protection that God promises us in Psalm 34:7? It is a spiritual fact that if God's angels are around us night and day, absolutely no evil spirits can survive in our presence.

It is obvious that the fear, that we are talking about is not the fear of being afraid of something or someone but, rather, the call to reverence God, to respect Him, and to walk in obedience to Him.

According to the law of Proverbs 8:13, "the fear of the Lord is to hate evil." When we fear God, we will love Him and do exactly what He says. Then all the shackles of witchcraft will be broken from off our lives, in His name.

Let us go deeper as we now look at the law of Proverbs 9, because this law helps us to fully understand that the fear we are examining is the beginning of wisdom and knowledge, which leads to deliverance.

> *The fear of the Lord is the beginning of wisdom: and the knowledge of the holy is understanding.* (Proverbs 9:10)

Now, when a person decides to fear or reverence the Lord, by walking in the spirit of obedience to all of His commandments, then and only then will God allow or send His angels to encamp around him. It is our obedience to divine authority that activates the law of Psalm 34:7. No amount of fasting and prayers or good works and services will cause God's angels to dwell around us.

The evil spirits of witchcraft and their curses will only and can only be defeated by the fear of the Lord. Yes! The fear of the Lord is also another powerful warfare weapon against the enemy. When we fear God, the Lord Himself will give His angel charge over us to keep according to the law of Psalm 91.

Now that we have this basic understanding of how to get God's angels to encamp around us, let us continue on our spiritual journey. We are going to see why the enemy is still wreaking havoc in many Christians' lives and homes by extension even while many are orally decreeing and declaring the word of the Lord.

Again, the law of Hosea 4:6 points us to the absolute truth as to the reason many within our churches will recite, decree, and declare the law of Psalm 34:7 and still suffer from the evil attacks of the enemy.

Many of God's people are ignorant of spiritual laws and principles. I was once a victim of witchcraft as I, too, was ignorant of the laws of God and how they work or operate. But when knowledge came, my deliverance also came, and the fear of the Lord enveloped my life, giving me the legal right for the law of Psalm 34:7 to be active in my life.

You can decree and declare, fast and pray, preach and teach, sow the seeds or give millions of dollars to the churches or charity, pay the tithes, speak in tongues, do all the good works possible, and God's angels still cannot encamp around you because the law of total obedience to divine authority is missing. It is imperative to know that wherever the presence of God is, there is liberty, and His angels will pitch their camp. The opposite is also true; whenever God withdraws His presence, we will have spiritual darkness. And wherever there is spiritual darkness, there are sicknesses, diseases, confusion, torment, chaos, and total wickedness as evil is present and God's angel cannot be there.

God's angels are also ministering spirits sent from the kingdom of God to serve us as the heirs of salvation, but these angels are unable to carry out their administrations in the lives of the disobedient. Remember, the law of Amos 3:3 clearly highlights the fact that two cannot walk together unless they are in agreement, and light and darkness cannot have fellowship. "Be ye not unequally yoked together with unbelievers: for what fellowship hath righteousness with unrighteousness? and what communion hath light with darkness?" (2 Corinthians 6:14).

I know some will argue that there are angels around them even while they are sleeping with the enemy, and they are correct. Because there are demonic angels around them—but *not* the ministering angels of the Lord. Hence, as Christians, we, therefore, need to test every spirit to see if it is the spirit of the living God before we accept any form of messages, laying on of the hands, or prophecies as there are many false and lying spirits within our churches; manipulating and deceiving many ignorant souls, according to the law of 1 John 4.

"Beloved, believe not every spirit, but try the spirits whether they are of God: because many false prophets are gone out into the world" (1 John 4:1).

The Advantages of God's angels around us

Let us take a moment and look at some of the advantages we will have if God's angels are encamping around us. The first thing we will witness is that Satan and his demons will become tormented and fearful. According to Matthew 8:29, "And, behold, they cried out, saying, What have we to do with thee, Jesus, thou Son of God? art thou come hither to torment us before the time?"

Demons will flee because they sense the presence of the Holy Spirit living in our lives, and they know that He is greater than them. As declared in 1 John 4:4, "Ye are of God, little children, and have overcome them: because greater is he that is in you than he that is in the world."

Absolutely no evil altars or evil gates will be able to rise up against us unless God gives permission, and it will only be for His glory, as in the case of Job.

> *Now there was a day when the sons of God came*
> *to present themselves before the Lord, and Satan also*
> *came among them. The Lord said to Satan, "From*
> *where have you come?" Satan answered the Lord*
> *and said, "From going to and fro on the earth, and*

from walking up and down on it." And the Lord said to Satan, "Have you considered my servant Job, that there is none like him on the earth, a blameless and upright man, who fears God and turns away from evil?" Then Satan answered the Lord and said, "Does Job fear God for no reason? Have you not put a hedge around him and his house and all that he has, on every side? You have blessed the work of his hands, and his possessions have increased in the land. But stretch out your hand and touch all that he has, and he will curse you to your face." And the Lord said to Satan, "Behold, all that he has is in your hand. Only against him do not stretch out your hand." So Satan went out from the presence of the Lord.

Now there was a day when his sons and daughters were eating and drinking wine in their oldest brother's house, and there came a messenger to Job and said, "The oxen were plowing and the donkeys feeding beside them, and the Sabeans fell upon them and took them and struck down the servants with the edge of the sword, and I alone have escaped to tell you."

While he was yet speaking, there came another and said, "The fire of God fell from heaven and burned up the sheep and the servants and consumed them, and I alone have escaped to tell you."

While he was yet speaking, there came another and said, "The Chaldeans formed three groups and made a raid on the camels and took them and struck down the servants with the edge of the sword, and I alone have escaped to tell you."

While he was yet speaking, there came another and said, "Your sons and daughters were eating and drinking wine in their oldest brother's house, and behold, a great wind came across the wilderness and struck the four corners of the house, and it fell upon the young people, and they are dead, and I alone have escaped to tell you."

Then Job arose and tore his robe and shaved his head and fell on the ground and worshiped.

And he said, "Naked I came from my mother's womb, and naked shall I return. The Lord gave, and the Lord has taken away; blessed be the name of the Lord."

In all this Job did not sin or charge God with wrong. (Job 1:6–22)

Many times, when people are suffering or being attacked by Satan and his demons, they will claim that it's a test from God. They will never confess that they are going against God's commandments, which now gives the enemy and his curses access and legal right to their lives (Proverbs 26:2).

They quickly confess that they are a "Job" being tested. But again the law of Proverbs 9 comes to prove how absolutely wrong they are. "As the bird by wandering, as the swallow by flying, so the curse causeless shall not come." Neither will they acknowledge the truth of Proverbs 26:27, "Whoso diggeth a pit shall fall therein: and he that rolleth a stone, it will return upon him." These people have totally forgotten the fact that Job was a righteous man before his test, and even during his test, absolutely nothing shifted his gaze from God because he remained faithful. How about you? Whenever we or our ancestors open doors of evil in our lives, it gives the enemies the legal right to attack, oppress, afflict, and inflict us in every department of our lives, especially our health.

See Lamentations 5:7, "Our fathers have sinned, *and are* not; and we have borne their iniquities" (emphasis added). However, thank God! If we confess our sins and the sins of our forefathers, our loving God will forgive us, and we will escape the punishment of our evil foundations. See Leviticus 26:40, "If they shall confess their iniquity, and the iniquity of their fathers, with their trespass which they trespassed against me, and that also they have walked contrary unto me."

If we dig deeper into the Scriptures, we will see the very same principle of obedience being used by Gideon. Gideon had to go up against his father's evil altar and tear it down. Because like many, this evil altar of his father's house was giving the enemies the upper hand even though Gideon was ignorant of his father's witchcraft altar. This evil altar blocked the Abrahamic blessings from flowing down to Gideon and the Israelites. God was angry! The curses were speaking, and Gideon and his people were in extreme poverty even though they were children of God as seen in the narrative below.

> *And the children of Israel did evil in the sight of the Lord: and the Lord delivered them into the hand of Midian seven years.*
>
> *And the hand of Midian prevailed against Israel: and because of the Midianites the children of Israel made them the dens which are in the mountains, and caves, and strong holds.*
>
> *And so it was, when Israel had sown, that the Midianites came up, and the Amalekites, and the children of the east, even they came up against them;*
>
> *And they encamped against them, and destroyed the increase of the earth, till thou come unto Gaza, and left no sustenance for Israel, neither sheep, nor ox, nor ass.*
>
> *For they came up with their cattle and their tents, and they came as grasshoppers for multitude; for both they and their camels were without number: and they entered into the land to destroy it.*
>
> *And Israel was greatly impoverished because of the Midianites; and the children of Israel cried unto the Lord.*
>
> *And it came to pass, when the children of Israel cried unto the Lord because of the Midianites,*

That the Lord sent a prophet unto the children of Israel, which said unto them, Thus saith the Lord God of Israel, I brought you up from Egypt, and brought you forth out of the house of bondage;

And I delivered you out of the hand of the Egyptians, and out of the hand of all that oppressed you, and drave them out from before you, and gave you their land;

And I said unto you, I am the Lord your God; fear not the gods of the Amorites, in whose land ye dwell: but ye have not obeyed my voice.

And there came an angel of the Lord and sat under an oak which was in Ophrah, that pertained unto Joash the Abiezrite: and his son Gideon threshed wheat by the winepress, to hide it from the Midianites.

And the angel of the Lord appeared unto him, and said unto him, The Lord is with thee, thou mighty man of valour.

And Gideon said unto him, Oh my Lord, if the Lord be with us, why then is all this befallen us? and where be all his miracles which our fathers told us of, saying, Did not the Lord bring us up from Egypt? but now the Lord hath forsaken us, and delivered us into the hands of the Midianites. (Judges 6:1–13)

From the narrative above, we get a vivid picture that because the angels of the Lord were not round about Gideon and his people, the spirits of robbery and poverty was upon them. This was as a result of the evil altar in Gideon's father's house.

And it came to pass the same night, that the Lord said unto him, Take thy father's young bullock, even the second bullock of seven years old, and throw down the altar of Baal that thy father hath, and cut down the grove that is by it:

And build an altar unto the Lord thy God upon the top of this rock, in the ordered place, and take the second bullock, and offer a burnt sacrifice with the wood of the grove which thou shalt cut down.

Then Gideon took ten men of his servants, and did as the Lord had said unto him: and so it was, because he feared his father's household, and the men of the city, that he could not do it by day, that he did it by night. (Judges 6:25–27)

Catch this! It was not until the altar was totally destroyed that God delivered the enemies into the hands of Gideon.

Judges 7:9; 23–25:

And it came to pass the same night, that the Lord said unto him, "Arise, get thee down unto the host; for I have delivered it into thine hand."

And the men of Israel gathered themselves together out of Naphtali, and out of Asher, and out of all Manasseh, and pursued after the Midianites.

And Gideon sent messengers throughout all mount Ephraim, saying, come down against the Midianites, and take before them the waters unto Bethbarah and Jordan. Then all the men of Ephraim gathered themselves together, and took the waters unto Bethbarah and Jordan.

And they took two princes of the Midianites, Oreb and Zeeb; and they slew Oreb upon the rock Oreb, and Zeeb they slew at the winepress of Zeeb, and pursued Midian, and brought the heads of Oreb and Zeeb to Gideon on the other side Jordan.

Gideon's father's evil altar was stopping God's angels from pitching their camps around them. Gideon and his people were suffering unnecessarily, like many of us today. Hence, when the spirit of knowledge descended upon him from God, Gideon listened and obeyed the voice of God in destroying the evil foundation of his father's house—so that God's angels could come and pitch their camps around him and his people for divine protection.

It is no different with us today; God's rules never change! According to the law of Matthew 24:35, "Heaven and earth shall pass away, but my words shall not pass away"

It is important for us to know spiritual rules and also to activate them in our daily lives so that these ministering angels of the Lord can encamp around us for our great protection and the shackles of witchcraft will be broken in Jesus' mighty name (Psalm 34:7).

Power will shift hands when God's angels encamp around us!

CHAPTER 6

Warring in the Spirit

For though we walk in the flesh, we do not
war after the flesh. (2 Corinthians 10:3)

Chapter 6 is a very powerful and interesting chapter as it is equipping
us with a deeper revelation as to how to truly gain the victory over the
enemy of witchcraft in the name of Jesus.

This spiritual law taken from 2 Corinthians 10:3 is an eye-
opener that comes to show us who our real enemies are. And even
though many ignorant people allow the devil and demons to use
their bodies to do evil unto others, our real enemies according to the
Scriptures are Satan and his demons (see Ephesians 6:12).

It is important to know that the invisible world is the world
where everything is conceived. It is the parenting world for our physical world. God does not always permit us to see into the invisible world. But the occult and the witchcraft practitioners rely upon
demons for their evil fulfillment of wickedness from the invisible
world.

In moving forward in identifying our real enemies, let us also
do what I will call a spiritual examination of the questions below, as
these questions will open our spiritual understanding as to how to
use the warfare weapon of spiritual knowledge against the enemies of

our destinies. As this is the hammer to truly break ourselves free from the shackles of witchcraft, in Jesus' name.

1. Are we really in a war?
2. What is this war about?
3. Where is this war happening?
4. Who are the real enemies?
5. How do we become victorious in the war?

Friends, it is obvious from 2 Corinthians 10:3 that we are in a war, but this war is not with other human beings like ourselves. It is with wicked, evil, demonic spirits, as described in the law of Ephesians 6:12. These evil spirits are our real enemies; we cannot see them with our physical eyes (unless God permits us to see them); but we can surely see and feel their evil works all around us as their physical manifestations take place. Though these are invisible disembodied beings, they can see and hear us, as they are intelligent creatures, according to the law of Matthew 12:43–45:

> *When an unclean spirit goes out of a man, he goes through dry places, seeking rest, and finds none. Then he says, "I will return to my house from which I came." And when he comes, he finds it empty, swept, and put in order. Then he goes and takes with him seven other spirits more wicked than himself, and they enter and dwell there; and the last state of that man is worse than the first. So shall it also be with this wicked generation.*

These unclean spirits can think, speak, and reason. They have and can show emotions, they have a will and self-awareness, and they can walk and respond. As a matter of fact, they are currently studying us, seeking to gain entrance into our lives through any form of disobedience to God's divine laws. See 1 John 3:4 and Proverbs 26:2 respectively. "Whosoever committeth sin transgresseth also the law:

for sin is the transgression of the law." "As the bird by wandering, as the swallow by flying, so the curse causeless shall not come."

Demons are man's real enemies, and they are all around—both in the invisible and the physical environment—living in many people's lives and homes, churches, offices, schools, old and abandoned buildings, and the like. And sadly, many people have legions of demons living inside them. This is the reason for their evil behaviors and affliction!

Continue to walk with me because this war that we are currently in is the same war from the beginning of creation as described below in The Revelation of Jesus the Christ.

> *And there was war in heaven: Michael and his angels fought against the dragon; and the dragon fought and his angels And prevailed not; neither was their place found any more in heaven.*
>
> *And the great dragon was cast out, that old serpent, called the Devil, and Satan, which deceiveth the whole world: he was cast out into the earth, and his angels were cast out with him.*
>
> *And I heard a loud voice saying in heaven, Now is come salvation, and strength, and the kingdom of our God, and the power of his Christ: for the accuser of our brethren is cast down, which accused them before our God day and night.*
>
> *And they overcame him by the blood of the Lamb, and by the word of their testimony; and they loved not their lives unto the death.*
>
> *Therefore rejoice, ye heavens, and ye that dwell in them. Woe to the inhabiters of the earth and of the sea! for the devil is come down unto you, having great wrath, because he knoweth that he hath but a short time.*
>
> *And when the dragon saw that he was cast unto the earth, he persecuted the woman which brought forth the man child.*

And to the woman were given two wings of a great eagle, that she might fly into the wilderness, into her place, where she is nourished for a time, and times, and half a time, from the face of the serpent.

And the serpent cast out of his mouth water as a flood after the woman, that he might cause her to be carried away of the flood.

And the earth helped the woman, and the earth opened her mouth, and swallowed up the flood which the dragon cast out of his mouth.

And the dragon was wroth with the woman, and went to make war with the remnant of her seed, which keep the commandments of God, and have the testimony of Jesus Christ. (Revelation 12:7–17)

It is the invisible war between good and evil, between God and Satan (Revelation 12:7–17). It is the war between us becoming obedient to divine authority or disobedient to the laws of God.

And if it seems evil unto you to serve the Lord, choose you this day whom ye will serve; whether the gods which your fathers served that were *on the other side of the flood, or the gods of the Amorites, in whose land ye dwell: but as for me and my house, we will serve the Lord.* (Joshua 24:15, emphasis added)

But where are the locations of this great war? Well, there are actually no physical addresses or locations or places where the war is taking place because, the truth is, this war is currently going on within each of our minds. It is a war that is taking place right now on the battlefields of our minds, even as you are reading this book. Therefore, the law of Philippians 2 commands us to take on the mind of Jesus so that we will be able to be victorious in this war. "Let this mind be in you, which was also in Christ Jesus" (Philippians 2:5). The minds are the real battlefields where this spiritual war between good and evil is raging every single day. We cannot run away from it as it is with us until the day we cease to be. Therefore, we are highly encouraged to be transformed by the renewing of our minds.

Romans chapter 12 and James chapter 1 encourage us not to take on the ways of this world, but instead, we should renew our minds by studying and meditating on the powerful words of God, and then we will hide it in our hearts so that we will not sin against Him. This type of lifestyle is really the only way to defeat the spirit of witchcraft and, by extension, the kingdom of darkness. "And be not conformed to this world: but be ye transformed by the renewing of your mind, that ye may prove what is that good, and acceptable, and perfect, will of God" (Romans 12:2). This transformation will come when we seek to study and do exactly what the Word of God dictates. See James 1:22, "But be ye doers of the word, and not hearers only, deceiving your own selves." It is a fact that many today are still asking various questions with regard to the invisible war that is constantly going on; but the main question that many still seek an answer for is, why is it that this war is against our minds?

The number one reason the war is against our minds is that it is with our minds that we serve the Lord. And the enemy, Satan, hates the Lord and wants our worship. So if he can destroy our minds, he can also destroy our relationships and our eternity with God. In Romans 7:25, Paul the apostle says, "I thank God through Jesus Christ our Lord. So then with the mind I myself serve the law of God; but with the flesh the law of sin." As a matter of fact, this enemy, Satan, hates all that God has created, and human beings (you and me) are his main enemies and targets. His mandate is to kill, steal, and destroy our divine destinies. Hence, we must fight back with the weapon of knowledge because greater is God inside us than the war that is going on, the battlefield of our minds.

And absolutely no evil counsels that are formed against us shall ever prosper because we have been given the divine authority by God through Jesus the Christ to trample upon all the fiery darts of the enemy without fear.

In Isaiah 54:17, we are informed, "No weapon that is formed against thee shall prosper; and every tongue that shall rise against thee in judgment thou shalt condemn. This is the heritage of the servants of the Lord, and their righteousness is of me, saith the Lord."

Jesus in Luke 10:19 solidifies Isaiah's declaration, "Behold, I give unto you power to tread on serpents and scorpions, and over all the power of the enemy: and nothing shall by any means hurt you." It is therefore important to note that when the spirit of knowledge is activated in our lives, the evil weapon of bewitchment cannot stand against us.

2 Timothy 1:7, further states that "God hath not given us the spirit of fear; but of power, and of love, and of a sound mind." But sadly, many people, and some of those who are Christians, are losing this war. They are losing on the battlefields of their minds because of three major enemies or strongholds.

The first enemy is ignorance.

The second enemy or stronghold is the evil spirit of fear. And, the third is the most dangerous of all, it is the spirit of disobedience to divine authority; pretty much like what happened in the story of Joshua.

See Joshua 6:16–19:

> And it came to pass at the seventh time, when the priests blew with the trumpets, Joshua said unto the people, Shout; for the Lord hath given you the city.
>
> And the city shall be accursed, even it, and all that are therein, to the Lord: only Rahab the harlot shall live, she and all that are with her in the house, because she hid the messengers that we sent.
>
> And ye, in any wise keep yourselves from the accursed thing, lest ye make yourselves accursed, when ye take of the accursed thing, and make the camp of Israel a curse, and trouble it.
>
> But all the silver, and gold, and vessels of brass and iron, are consecrated unto the Lord: they shall come into the treasury of the Lord.

Achan was overpowered by the enemy, Satan, on the battle-field of his mind. He disobeyed God's commands and took of the accursed.

See also Joshua 7:7–25:

> *And Joshua said, Alas, O Lord God, wherefore hast thou at all brought this people over Jordan, to deliver us into the hand of the Amorites, to destroy us? would to God we had been content, and dwelt on the other side Jordan!*
>
> *O Lord, what shall I say, when Israel turneth their backs before their enemies!*
>
> *For the Canaanites and all the inhabitants of the land shall hear of it, and shall environ us round, and cut off our name from the earth: and what wilt thou do unto thy great name?*
>
> *And the Lord said unto Joshua, Get thee up; wherefore liest thou thus upon thy face?*
>
> *Israel hath sinned, and they have also transgressed my covenant which I commanded them: for they have even taken of the accursed thing, and have also stolen, and dissembled also, and they have put it even among their own stuff.*
>
> *Therefore the children of Israel could not stand before their enemies, but turned their backs before their enemies, because they were accursed: neither will I be with you any more, except ye destroy the accursed from among you.*
>
> *Up, sanctify the people, and say, Sanctify yourselves against tomorrow: for thus saith the Lord God of Israel, There is an accursed thing in the midst of thee, O Israel: thou canst not stand before thine enemies, until ye take away the accursed thing from among you.*
>
> *In the morning therefore ye shall be brought according to your tribes: and it shall be, that the*

tribe which the Lord taketh shall come according to the families thereof; and the family which the Lord shall take shall come by households; and the household which the Lord shall take shall come man by man.

And it shall be, that he that is taken with the accursed thing shall be burnt with fire, he and all that he hath: because he hath transgressed the covenant of the Lord, and because he hath wrought folly in Israel.

So Joshua rose up early in the morning, and brought Israel by their tribes; and the tribe of Judah was taken:

And he brought the family of Judah; and he took the family of the Zarhites: and he brought the family of the Zarhites man by man; and Zabdi was taken

And he brought his household man by man; and Achan, the son of Carmi, the son of Zabdi, the son of Zerah, of the tribe of Judah, was taken.

And Joshua said unto Achan, My son, give, I pray thee, glory to the Lord God of Israel, and make confession unto him; and tell me now what thou hast done; hide it not from me.

And Achan answered Joshua, and said, Indeed I have sinned against the Lord God of Israel, and thus and thus have I done:

When I saw among the spoils a goodly Babylonish garment, and two hundred shekels of silver, and a wedge of gold of fifty shekels weight, then I coveted them, and took them; and, behold, they are hid in the earth in the midst of my tent, and the silver under it.

So Joshua sent messengers, and they ran unto the tent; and, behold, it was hid in his tent, and the silver under it.

*And they took them out of the midst of the
tent, and brought them unto Joshua, and unto all
the children of Israel, and laid them out before the
Lord.*

*And Joshua, and all Israel with him, took
Achan the son of Zerah, and the silver, and the garment, and the wedge of gold, and his sons, and his
daughters, and his oxen, and his asses, and his sheep,
and his tent, and all that he had: and they brought
them unto the valley of Achor.*

*And Joshua said, Why hast thou troubled us?
the Lord shall trouble thee this day. And all Israel
stoned him with stones, and burned them with fire,
after they had stoned them with stones.*

Many people are busy warring in the physical as they curse their
neighbors, fight with the kids, divorce the wife/husband, kick the
dogs, practice continuous gossiping, backbiting, and bewitchment of
one another, and become totally disrespectful to God and His divine
authority. These sinful activities are powerful weapons in the hands
of the enemy to continue his evil mandate on the battlefield of our
minds. But can we really become victorious in this war? *Yes!* Anyone
who chooses to listen and follow the Lord's instructions is victorious
in this war.

For Jesus the Christ has disarmed this enemy on the battlefield
at Calvary's cross. "And having spoiled principalities and powers, he
made a shew of them openly, triumphing over them in it" (Colossians
2:15).

Revelation 12:11 also boldly highlights the fact that we are
overcomers in this war: "And they overcame him by the blood of the
Lamb, and by the word of their testimony, and they loved not their
lives unto the death." Jesus the Christ had entered the battlefield and
took back the keys of hell and the grave from our enemy, Satan. See
Romans 6:10 NLT, "When he died, he died once to break the power
of sin. But now that he lives, he lives for the glory of God."

Jesus has already stripped the powers from principalities and powers, and the gates of hell can *never* prevail against the true followers of Christ. See Matthew 16:17–19, "And I say also unto thee, That thou art Peter, and upon this rock I will build my church; and the gates of hell shall not prevail against it."

Therefore, when a true child of God fights, he fights in the spirit.

He fights from the third heavens. See Ephesians 2:6, "And hath raised us up together, and made us sit together in heavenly places in Christ Jesus."

He fights via fasting and prayer. See Matthew 17:21, "Howbeit this kind goeth not out but by prayer and fasting."

He fights by walking in total obedience to the Word of God. See John 14:15, "If ye love me, keep my commandments."

He fights in opposition to the enemies while activating the law of Proverbs 11:9b and Psalm 119:11. "An hypocrite with *his* mouth destroyeth his neighbour: but through knowledge shall the just be delivered" (emphasis added). "Thy word have I hid in mine heart, that I might not sin against thee."

We, the followers of Jesus the Christ, know that the flesh profits nothing; hence, we refuse to activate the works of the flesh in our lives, according to the law of Galatians 5.

> *Now the works of the flesh are manifest, which are these; adultery, fornication, uncleanness, lasciviousness, idolatry, witchcraft, hatred, variance, emulations, wrath, strife, seditions, heresies, envyings, murders, drunkenness, revellings, and such like: of the which I tell you before, as I have also told you in time past, that they which do such things shall not inherit the kingdom of God.* (Galatians 5:19–21)

We also know that the flesh cannot pull down strongholds on the battlefield of our minds.

> For the weapons of our warfare are not carnal, but mighty through God to the pulling down of strong holds. Casting down imaginations, and every high thing that exalteth itself against the knowledge of God, and bringing into captivity every thought to the obedience of Christ. (2 Corinthians 10:4–5)

The flesh is weak in the realm of the spirit, so the Word of the Lord is our only weapon! As I make my way to our final destination, I want us to pull the law of Philippians 2 into focus because this is a very powerful warfare weapon that all believers must have on the battlefield of their minds. "Let this mind be in you, which was also in Christ Jesus" (Philippians 2:5).

When we take on the mind of Christ, absolutely no witchcraft, no powers, or any other forms of wickedness from Satan's kingdom can stand against us. Hence, we will win the war in the name of Jesus the Christ. Spiritual warfare is not a joke; we must put the law of James 1 into our everyday practices and live a victorious life that will break the shackles of witchcraft from our lives and destinies. "But be ye doers of the word, and not hearers only, deceiving your own selves" (James 1:22). Then every curse that is working against you from any evil altar will be revoked by the powerful blood of Jesus. In addition, the wisdom of the household witches will be converted to foolishness in the name of Jesus the Christ.

You will begin to live a happy, peaceful, victorious, and blessed life in God as you maintain your powerful deliverance through consistently studying and applying the Word of God in your life. God blesses you. Amen!

Powerful Warfare Prayers for Deliverance

Pray these prayers with seriousness and a strong belief in the power of God.

Make sure that you repent of all known and unknown sins before engaging in this warfare section. Note, however, that a life of obedience to divine authority is the only life of victory in Jesus Christ (see John 14:15).

1. No weapon that is formed against me and my family shall prosper because of the powerful blood of Jesus in Jesus' name.
2. It is written, I overcome Satan by the blood of Jesus Christ and the powerful word of my testimony.
3. I scatter all evil altars with the weapon of my warfare in the powerful name of Jesus Christ.
4. I send the hammer of God into every evil altar, cauldron, and everywhere my name and that of my family members have been called for evil.
5. According to Jeremiah 23:29, the Word of the Lord is like fire; let the powerful Word of the Lord burn to ashes every witchcraft hand that is lifted against my destiny in the mighty name of Jesus Christ.

6. I cancel all witchcraft dreams and break and burn all evil covenants in the name of Jesus Christ.

7. God, let the plans of the enemies backfire in the name of Jesus Christ.

8. For Jesus the Christ has disarmed principalities and powers, so let the powerful finger of God arise and write the judgment of the wicked witches and wizards that are working against me and my family in the name of Jesus Christ.

9. Lord, according to the law of Isaiah 7:7, the curses of evil altars shall not stand against me and my destiny, neither shall they come to pass in my life in the name of Jesus Christ.

10. The angel of the Lord encamps around them that fear the Lord. Lord, I reverence You, now let Your angels stay around me in the name of Jesus the Christ.

11. I release the blood of Jesus against all ancestral spirits in the mighty name of Jesus the Christ.

12. I command every family altar to open up and receive the fire of God and be destroyed in the name of Jesus the Christ.

13. Let all evil witchcraft candles burning for my sake be put to shame in the name of Jesus the Christ.

14. Witchcraft burial for my sake, return to sender in the powerful name of Jesus the Christ.

15. From henceforth, let no man trouble me, for within my body, I bear the marks of the Lord Jesus Christ. Blood of Jesus, arise and wash off all evil witchcraft marks from my divine destiny in the name of Jesus the Christ.

16. I use the sword of the Spirit, and I dismantle all evil legs that are walking into my destiny in the name of Jesus the Christ.

17. Let every Goliath on the battlefield of my mind be put to death in the name of Jesus the Christ.

18. I speak death to the spirit of jealousy in the name of Jesus the Christ.

19. Every coffin spirit, die by fire in the name of Jesus the Christ.
20. I am more than a conqueror in the name of Jesus the Christ.
21. Let all evil hands dry up in the name of Jesus the Christ.
22. Spirit of oppression, eat your own flesh and drink your own blood in the name of Jesus the Christ.
23. For God has not given me a spirit of fear, let every spirit of fear scatter by fire in the name of Jesus the Christ.
24. And God shall keep me in perfect peace because my mind is stayed on Him; therefore, let all enemies of my peace be restless in the name of Jesus the Christ.
25. Spirit of worries, return to your sender in the powerful name of Jesus the Christ.
26. I stone the spirit of Balaam in the name of Jesus the Christ.
27. I command every backward spirit to catch his owner in the name of Jesus the Christ.
28. Spirit of rejection, I bind and scatter you in the name of Jesus the Christ.
29. Let the tormentors be tormented and the arrestors be arrested by the blood of Jesus the Christ in the name of Jesus.
30. Owners of evil loads, carry your own loads in the name of Jesus the Christ.
31. Spirit of procrastination, fall and die in the name of Jesus the Christ.
32. I decree and declare that my hands are on the necks of my enemies in the name of Jesus the Christ.
33. Lord, Your Word declares that no good thing will be withheld from me because I am walking uprightly with You in the name of Jesus the Christ.
34. Let all my Pharaohs be drowned in the sea of confusion in the name of Jesus the Christ.
35. You my Haman get busy with useless assignments in the mighty name of Jesus the Christ.

36. Let all my Judas' commit suicide in the name of Jesus the Christ.

37. Every yoke of bondage, be broken by the blood of Jesus in the mighty name of Jesus the Christ.

38. I command every demonic idols to return to Satan in the powerful name of Jesus the Christ.

39. Evil spirits of lack, stagnation, poverty, and confusion, scatter by fire in the powerful name of Jesus the Christ.

40. Any spirit that is causing me to sin, fall and die out of my life in the name of Jesus the Christ.

41. You my tongue receive hot coals from the altar of God in the name of Jesus the Christ.

42. I bind and cast out every restless spirit out of every department of my life in the name of Jesus the Christ.

43. Let every spirit of division and every altar of scattering that is lifted against my family be roasted by the judgment fire of the living God in the name of Jesus the Christ.

44. Unstoppable hands of God, hug around me and my beautiful family in the name of Jesus the Christ.

45. I command my spirit to love the Lord and walk in obedience to all of His divine instructions in the name of Jesus the Christ.

46. Sprit of the living God, catapult me into my divine destiny of greatness in the name of Jesus the Christ.

47. Let the hands of all evil priests be put to confusion for my sake in the name of Jesus the Christ.

48. I scatter all salt altars, and I break their covenants in the name of Jesus the Christ.

49. Let all snail anointment and vagabond spirit be roasted in the name of Jesus the Christ.

50. Powerful hands of God, arise and destroy all hidden and unbroken curses of my father's house in the name of Jesus the Christ.

51. Let all evil cries of my family idol be silenced by the powerful blood of Jesus the Christ in Jesus' mighty name.

52. I command all demons and their works to scatter out of every department of my life by the power in the blood of Jesus in the name of Jesus the Christ.

53. Spirit of infirmity on the battlefield of life, be roasted by Holy Ghost fire in the name of Jesus Christ.

54. Powers of the night, be overpowered in the name of Jesus Christ.

55. I send the spirit of ambushment against every strongman and woman of my destiny, and I command them to turn against themselves in the name of Jesus Christ.

56. I decree and declare that I shall not die but live to declare the works of the Lord in the land of the living in the name of Jesus the Christ.

57. I shall lend and not borrow in the name of Jesus Christ.

58. I plead the blood of Jesus against all evil decrees programmed against my life in the name of Jesus Christ.

59. I plead the blood of Jesus against every spirit of failure in the name of Jesus the Christ.

60. I close all evil doors opened for my sake in the name of Jesus the Christ.

61. Every curse of the dust, return to sender in the name of Jesus the Christ.

62. I command every demonic holes in my pockets to be sealed up now by the blood of Jesus in the name of Jesus Christ.

63. Spiritual robbers of my divine blessings, be roasted by Holy Ghost fire in the name of Jesus Christ.

64. Every power that seeks to overpower me, be disgraced in the name of Jesus Christ.

65. I break all witchcraft shackles off my life and that of my sleep in the powerful blood of Jesus Christ.

66. Let the cleansing blood of Jesus Christ wash away every evil mark of the water spirit from my sleep in the mighty name of Jesus Christ.

67. I command every unbroken curse to be broken now by the blood of Jesus Christ.

68. I command every evil river flowing into my sleep to dry up in the powerful name of Jesus Christ.

69. Stubborn enemies of my sleep, die in the name of Jesus Christ.

70. Ancestral spirits crying against my sleep, be silenced by the speaking blood of Jesus Christ in the name of Jesus.

71. I command every evil river flowing into my finance to dry up in the powerful name of Jesus Christ.

72. Stubborn enemies of my success, die in the name of Jesus Christ.

73. I decree and declare by the speaking blood of Jesus the Christ that on the first day of my fast, all the enemies will be engulfed by the spirit of trembling in the name of Jesus.

74. I decree and declare that I have great peace because I love the laws of the Lord in the name of Jesus.

75. I decree and declare that I am always dressed in the armour of the Lord, and I am ready for battle in the victorious name of Jesus the Christ.

76. I decree and declare that my heart is merry and my health is excellent in the name of Jesus the Christ.

77. I command all witchcraft curses over my destiny to be broken in the name of Jesus.

78. I speak life into my destiny now in the name of Jesus.

79. I command the spirit of jealousy to run mad in the name of Jesus.

80. Lord, let your angels encamp around me and my family in the name of Jesus.

81. I command my spirit-man to walk in the way of the Lord and defeat all the plans of the enemies in the name of Jesus the Christ.

82. I decree and declare that the weapon of my warfare is not carnal but mighty in battles for the pulling down of demonic strongholds in the powerful name of Jesus the Christ.

83. I activate by faith the laws of blessings and power over my life, my health, my home, my family, and my finances in the powerful name of Jesus.

84. Evil cords of envy burn to ashes and scatter in the victorious name of Jesus the Christ.

85. I send the blood of Jesus the Christ against every spiritual ties of bewitchment in the powerful name of Jesus the Christ.

86. I decree and declare by the blood of Jesus the Christ that the evil counsels of the enemies against my marriage shall not stand nor come to pass in my family in the name of Jesus.

87. Every evil counsel from the kingdom of darkness backfires by Holy Ghost fire in the powerful name of Jesus.

88. Spirits of wisdom, knowledge, and obedience overshow me and my household in the name of Jesus.

89. I trample upon every witchcraft evil counsel that is set against me and my destiny in the mighty name of Jesus the Christ.

90. Oh Lord my God, my Redeemer, and my Savior, let Your ministering angels rain fire and brimstones upon all the enemies of my peace in the name of Jesus the Christ.

91. By the blood of Jesus the Christ, the battles have been won, and I am free in the mighty name of Jesus.

92. Full authority has been given to me according to the law of Luke 10:19; therefore, I trample upon all curses, evil altars, witchcraft spirits, marine spirits, and ancestral spirits in the name of Jesus the Christ.

93. Like Gideon, power has shifted hands and the angels of God make their dwelling place around me, in the name of Jesus.

94. I command the spirit of oppression to scatter into torment in the mighty name of Jesus the Christ.

95. Evil spirit of Pharoah in my life, scatter into destruction in the mighty name of Jesus.

96. I burn and scatter every plan of the enemy to keep me in bondage in the powerful name of Jesus the Christ.

97. Fire of the living God, kill all of Pharaoh's firstborns in the mighty name of Jesus the Christ.

98. Let the wheels of Pharaoh's chariots be smashed and broken by the power of the living God in the name of Jesus.

99. I decree and declare that the enemies shall drink their own blood in the mighty name of Jesus the Christ.

100. All glory, power, honor, and praise be unto the victorious Lamb of God, for the battles have been won in the name of Jesus.

101. Leftover curses from my father and mother's houses, burn to ashes and scatter from my life in the powerful name of Jesus the Christ.

102. Fire of the living God, burn every witchcraft curses and the evil effects of their altars over my life in the mighty name of Jesus the Christ.

103. By the blood of Jesus the Christ, I command "this kind" to come out of my life and the lives of my children in the victorious name of Jesus the Christ.

104. Every weapon that is formed against me on my journey with God shall not prosper, in the name of Jesus.

105. The Word of the Lord is established in my home; therefore, the evil spirit of witchcraft cannot enter in the name of Jesus.

106. I speak against Balaam's twenty-one evil altars in the name of Jesus the Christ.

107. Rain of affliction falls upon every evil altar where my name and that of my family members have been summoned for evil in the name of Jesus the Christ.

108. I break every evil covenant of my father's and mother's houses that is speaking against my divine success in the deliverance name of Jesus the Christ.

109. Lord God of my salvation, let the weapon of the wicked be their downfall in the name of Jesus the Christ.

110. Powerful blood of Jesus, arise and answer the evil voice of the powers of the night that are speaking against my rest in the name of Jesus the Christ.

111. Lord, I praise you that the sun shall not smite me by day nor the moon by night in the name of Jesus the Christ.

112. Spirit of selfishness, get out of my life in the name of Jesus the Christ.

113. Lord, like Jeshosophat, allow me and my family to gather the spoils of the enemies in the powerful name of Jesus the Christ.

114. Let the anointing on my life, mingled with the blood of Jesus the Christ, destroy the arrows of affliction in the name of Jesus.

115. Hammer and fire of the living God, locate and destroy all crossroad altars, where my pictures and name have been planted for evil in the mighty name of Jesus the Christ.

116. Spirit of amputation on my life, burn to ashes and scatter in the name of Jesus the Christ.

117. Let the blood of Jesus the Christ flush out every spirit of infirmity out of every organ of my body in the name of Jesus the Christ.

118. O Lord of vengeance, let the heads of Ahab's children be cut off and his household scatter into confusion in the name of Jesus the Christ.

119. O God of my salvation, let me and my blessed family dwell in the hallow of God's hands in the name of Jesus the Christ. Amen!

THE END

ABOUT THE AUTHOR

Sweda had been under severe demonic witchcraft attacks. But spiritual ignorance was the fuel that the enemy weaponized and used to almost destroy her life.

The Bible is clear, it is through knowledge and its application that the author (the captive) was set free (Proverbs 11:9b).

Therefore, the author now listens to the powerful voice of God in writing books about the biblical principles that she had used to become totally free from the shackles of witchcraft.

It was Sweda's personal pledge made to God that if He had set her free from the powers of witchcraft, which was strangulating her sleep, her family, and her finances, she would thereby encourage others who are held down by these demonic forces to be freed also.

She came to realize that millions of people in the world today are under the evil power of witchcraft, and they are crying out for help and for a permanent solution. Therefore, the Holy Spirit also led her to write a powerful book entitled *Overthrowing the Evil Spirit of Sleeplessness*. Sweda is a teacher by profession and has studied at the graduate level. She was born in Jamaica. She also writes devotionals and currently lives with her family and their dog, Chase. She loves the Lord with all her heart, and it is Sweda's desire to see men and women, boys and girls be set free from the shackles of witchcraft in the victorious name of our Lord and Savior Jesus the everlasting Christ.

Milton Keynes UK
Ingram Content Group UK Ltd.
UKHW010931050224
437294UK00001B/183